The
Wage Slave's
Toolkit

Gary Gade

Vole Guides

The Wage Slave's Toolkit
by Gary Gade

Editor: Zack Diston
Proofreader: Diane Yee
Compositor: Sylvia Thorpe
Cover: Questing Vole Press

Contents

CHAPTER 1

Managing Your Time

The same scene plays in thousands of offices every day: someone mentally drifts away from an afternoon meeting asking, *Have I done anything important with my time today?* If you've been asking yourself that question, it's likely because you're not good at managing time. That's unfortunate—the most valuable asset in your career (and maybe in your life) is time.

Time is wasted in a long list of ways. Doing the wrong work. Doing the right work at the wrong time. Dwelling on personal issues. Socializing. The problem is so commonplace that legions of time-management consultants are ready to help you use time more effectively. They bill millions each year to organizations, teams, and individuals. These consultants are often competent and well intentioned, but their presentations and methods are usually geared for the dumbest guy in the room, so they, ironically, waste a lot of time.

Fortunately, there's a simpler approach to transforming your day. Following three simple rules will change how you use your time:

- The 80/20 rule—spend most of your time doing only the work that matters most.

- Achieving flow—enter a state in which you're mentally the most agile, and maintain that state.

- Signal your availability—let people know when you don't want to be interrupted.

1

Practice all three rules together, every day, and your productivity will rocket, bringing you new successes and less stress because you learned how to be more thoughtful and intentional about how to use your time.

Rule 1: The 80/20 Rule

Economists call it the Pareto principle, statisticians call it the power law, but most people call it the 80/20 rule (or, with gravitas, the law of the vital few). For our purposes, it means spending most of your time doing the most important 20% of your work.

Examine every task on your to-do list, every project, every person, every client, and every email to determine whether it's a 20%er (vital, interesting, or strategic) or an 80%er (less important, trivial, or dying of neglect). Every time some new bit of work comes your way, decide immediately whether it's a 20%er or 80%er. Allocate your time by mentally pigeonholing every blip on your radar. Be ruthless, or you're likely to waste too much time on 80%ers.

In general, never spend more than half of your time in the 80% pile. If you do find yourself mired in the 80% swamp, then do one of the following:

- **Delegate.** Business-speak for "Make someone else do it." Let a direct report or staff member take care of it. Test the waters by delegating simple tasks at first—writing first drafts or creating PowerPoint slides, for example.

- **Outsource.** Hire a vendor or consultant to do the work.

- **Automate.** If you're technically inclined, use Excel, Access, or Microsoft Office macros to automate the work. Or write shell scripts in PowerShell (Microsoft Windows) or bash (Mac OS X and Linux).

Rule 2: Achieve Flow

Now that you know *what* to work on (the 20%ers), it's time to decide *when*. And that would be the time period when you're most likely to achieve *flow*. Flow is a mental peak in which a person is immersed and focused fully on an activity. It's the single-minded harnessing of emotions in the service of reaching a goal. At work, you're in flow when you solve problems easily, work flies off your desk, and your skills are the equal of the challenges. Flow increases your satisfaction and sense of accomplishment. You're in tune, in the moment, and ready for whatever comes next.

Flow is one of life's great feelings, but learning how to gain a state where previously frightening challenges take on an aspect of relaxed ease requires great conscious effort, patience, and discipline. It is you who must transform, and that takes work. If you're having trouble reaching flow, or if you want to learn more about it, read Mihaly Csikszentmihalyi's seminal and popular book, *Flow: The Psychology of Optimal Experience.* Moderate to heavy internet users often find it hard to achieve flow, as explained in Nicholas Carr's *The Shallows: What the Internet Is Doing to Our Brains.*

Everyone has their own best times for achieving flow, and those times can vary day to day—it might be mid-morning today and early evening tomorrow. My own flow window occurs at the same time every day, in the early morning. At 6:30 a.m., I glance at my to-do list, apply the 80/20 rule, and jump into my work. Three minutes after I start writing, I'm in flow.

If you don't know exactly when your flow window occurs, then experiment and reflect. The 80/20 rule is only part of using your time effectively, and it works best not when used in isolation but as a precursor to flow.

Flow also happens outside the workplace, especially during learning, sports, games, singing, music-making, and spiritual pursuits.

Protecting Flow

If you're in flow and functioning at a high level, knocking off 20%ers, it's natural to want to protect that feeling. Step one is to turn off your phone, log off your email and messaging accounts, and silence any other noise-makers for the duration of your flow window. (This step has the added benefit of reducing stress. Stress impedes flow.) Cutting your electronic umbilical for a half hour might trigger some discomfort, but it'll pass as soon as you get focused.

Disconnecting your gadgets eliminates major distractions, but still leaves you vulnerable to face-to-face ambushes. You can mitigate these surprises by saying the magic word:

"No."

Saying "No" in a "Yes" society is tough, but is required if you want to reclaim and defend your time.

An example: you're sitting in your office, in flow and working on a 20%er. Then your boss or a coworker walks in looking for your help with some dreary task ("Would you proofread this report/disinfect my computer/handle this complaint?"). Regardless of your relationship with the interloper, the correct answer is almost always "No." Your first impulse may be "Yes," but invoke free will and self-censorship so that it comes out "No." You can soften the blow by couching it as, "Yes, I can help you but not just now. I'll come see you at 11:30 and we'll tackle it. Is that OK?" Almost always the response is "Yes." The person walks away and you suffer only a ten-second interruption to your train of thought during the most important part of your day.

Another way to minimize disruptions is to leave your normal office space and hole up in an empty office or conference room, if available. Even if you have your own office, a temporary relocation might work better than closing your door. The best havens are on the other side of the building.

Rule 3: Signal Your Availability

Do your colleagues feel comfortable knocking on your door or leaning in to your cubicle at any time? If so, find overt ways to let them know when you're not to be interrupted, or when you're somewhat open to being interrupted. A favorite system among time-management consultants is color-coded signaling: workers post conspicuous green, yellow, or red flags (or signs or velcro strips or whatever) on their workspaces, changing them throughout the day, as needed. Each color represents a level of availability. Green = OK, feel free to stop by unannounced; yellow = busy, important interruptions only; and red = stop, stay away unless you're my boss with an issue of great importance. This system can work remarkably well, particularly when people don't overuse the red signal.

If this system won't work for you, you'll have to come up with something else that fits with your work environment and office politics. Some people try to use body language (facial expressions, posture, and so on) to keep others at bay but that usually doesn't work because nonverbal cues are easily misinterpreted (and anyway, you're likely to lose track of your posture when you're in flow). In any case, your system must be readily observable or people will have already broken your flow by poking in their heads asking, "Are you free?"

Chapter 2

Building Confidence

Self confidence, a key ingredient in a successful life and career, is the belief in self that lets you *envision* mastering the skills needed to accomplish interesting and challenging goals. If you have strong self confidence, others feel it, know it, and want to include you. If you're not self confident, the reverse is true: others sense it and question you.

Confidence is a skill, and developing it is a long-term, step-by-step process that requires effort and the right attitude. Let's start.

Envision Future States

To start building your confidence, think about where you want to go, beginning with an honest accounting of where you are. Look at your life: your skills, responsibilities, salary, business, family, friends, satisfaction, turmoil—everything. Make no excuses and assign no blame. Accept that you're here because of your own choices, and not because you were betrayed by others or raised by incompetent parents.

Only after you own your current situation can you start to think about the future that you want to create. Ponder who you want to be in a few years. Choose a horizon that's not too far away, but distant enough to let you genuinely better your life, with the right effort. Think positively about the new you, say, five years hence: your future attitude, responsibilities, skills, status, and inner state. Don't indulge in negative thinking about the outcomes (that's a trait of people who lack self confidence).

Don't let these future possible states become fleeting ideas. Invest in them, be specific, and write them down. You're going to return to them in the coming years to reflect on them.

Ponder Your Awful Past

Face the monsters under your bed, cut them loose, and move on. Dealing with your past lets you avoid negative thinking in envisioning future outcomes. Usually one, two, or three things—persons or events—in your past can best explain how you arrived at your current level of confidence. Slay the monsters in two steps:

1. **Write about them.** Write them down as you would record them in a private diary. Articulate the people, places, and events that you believe explain your current lack of confidence. Confront what you're trying not to think about. How did that happen? Could it have been avoided? What did you learn, if anything? Now ask yourself, "All this time later, do those things matter?" They *feel* like they do, but do they really? Almost always, the answer is no or not much. Such misfortunes, when viewed clearly, almost always shrink in perspective.

2. **Talk about them.** Find at least one confidante (but no more than two or three) who knows you personally and professionally. Share with them what you identified in your writings. Talking at least a little bit about monsters reduces their power and makes them things that you can learn from. Try to laugh at them therapeutically. Recall James Thurber's observation that "humor is emotional chaos remembered in tranquility."

Be Useful to Others

In addition to positioning yourself mentally to grow your self confidence, you must change your behavior. Start by helping others and volunteering your time. At work, help two or three colleagues who need your assistance. In your community, there's no shortage of opportunities to lend a hand. Looking outside yourself and helping others is the first big behavioral step in terms of self confidence. Being useful to others:

- Is fun, the right thing to do, and an end in itself

- Lets the people who receive your help affirm your worth and expertise, often in small or subtle ways

- Invigorates you by letting you watch others chase their goals, reminding you of your own journey

- Lets you do for others what you're about to start doing for yourself

Small Wins, Small Rewards

After gaining a few bumps in confidence by helping others, turn your focus inward by looking for meaningful incremental steps past your current level of performance. Take small steps that yield small wins for small rewards. Don't immerse yourself in your five-year dream yet (that comes later). Consider measurable activities and tasks for which you've plateaued: distance running, backgammon playing, spreadsheet modeling, novel writing, stock picking, whatever. Everyone plateaus.

Now ask yourself not what you can do to become expert or celebrated (even if that's your long-term goal), but what you can do to effect a small improvement. Can you eat, sleep, practice, study, or schedule differently? Think of a legitimate, meaningful, incremental goal that you can actually achieve. And then change your routines and whatever else you must to reach that incremental step.

For each small win, give yourself something—not a celebration, but a small, measured reward (something that you usually deny yourself). You earned it.

For several months, define incremental strides, achieve them, and reward them. When you become comfortable with these small measured improvements, you're ready for the next step.

Leave Negativeland

After making behavioral progress, remove negative events and negative people as much as possible from your life. Think about the times during the preceding year when you felt the worst, whether or not you were the cause of that negativity. Write them down—the tasks, projects, situations, contexts, and people. Be honest and fluent, because these irritants are targets to be fully or partially removed from your life to the extent possible.

By taking complementary actions, you can create a positive context that boosts your self confidence significantly:

- **Avoid the negative.** Choose a few of the major negativity triggers from your list and then project them into the future. Ask yourself whether you must encounter these tasks and people. Then ask whether you can avoid or reduce contact with these catalysts. Strive to reduce the amount of time that you spend doing those things or being with those people.

- **Pursue the positive.** Think about the times during the preceding year when you felt the most happy and engaged. Which tasks and people were involved? Ask yourself whether there's a reasonable way to increase their role in your life. Your goal is to bring closer to you stimulants for positive thinking.

Visualize Success

The next step is to learn how to visualize yourself achieving a goal. This technique is popular among overachievers, who regularly visualize themselves being successful: surfing big waves, graduating from medical school, winning an election, sitting in a new corner office, and so on. Every day, spend time alone quietly running a detailed movie in your mind of yourself doing what you're trying to achieve. Watch that movie regularly and edit it when necessary to match your current reality. Soon enough, this mental documentary will become a clarifying filter for your daily behaviors, prompting you to ask yourself whether what you're doing will actually help you reach the envisioned outcome.

Use your movie to stay focused. Watch it a lot—at least five minutes a day—but not obsessively (that's just daydreaming). Start with only one goal, and then when you become comfortable in the director's chair, focus on multiple outcomes.

Fail Better

The next step is to plan for failure. You're going to experience setbacks and failures as you try to build confidence and chase new goals. You won't see failure coming, so your surprise will make it hurt. Preparing for failure softens the blow and makes you less likely to dwell on it:

- **Admit it.** Acknowledge failure but recognize it as only a setback, not a fatal flaw or tragic mistake (which are rare outside of literature and popular culture).

- **Own it.** Think about it. Write about it reflectively. Talk about it a little with at least one person you trust. If it's an interesting setback, learn from it.

And then pick yourself up and keep moving forward. Improving yourself, building confidence, and chasing goals is an erratic process. You want a positive trend. Think about the price of oil—always trending up but with significant ups and downs along the way. The slope of your own trend line depends more on how you handle the down moments than the up moments.

Self Assess

It's time to pause and assess your progress critically. The purpose of the preceding steps was to make you comfortable with incremental improvements in your confidence. Look back over the steps that you've taken—helping others, removing negativity, and so on—and describe how well you've progressed over the last few months.

Is your daily level of self-confidence clearly greater now than when you started? Building confidence is a long-term nonlinear process, so it's normal to feel that you've made a little progress but nearly enough. If that's the case, cycle through the entire process again over the next few months, starting with envisioning future states. You may have to cycle repeatedly until you become comfortable with the behaviors that increase confidence.

When you're consistently making incremental progress, when it makes sense, and when you like it, then you're finished assessing and cycling, and ready for the next step.

Step Up Your Game

It's time to accelerate the confidence-building process by moving from incremental goals to ambitious goals. Bring your five-year dream back into focus and ask yourself what has to happen—three or four milestones—to get from where you are now to where you want to be in five years. These milestones are your new goals.

Along your newly accelerated journey, all the preceding steps are still important, but some more so than others, especially avoiding negativity and visualizing success. People are going to notice that you're confidently chasing larger goals, and they're going to block you, gossip about you, and tell you that you won't succeed. But you can prepare by predicting who those people will be and avoiding them.

In tandem with avoiding negativity, visualize reaching every milestone. Where are you? What are you going? Who are you talking to? What are you wearing? Watch your movie every day.

Follow this advice every day and soon you'll be making significant steps forward.

Big Wins, Big Rewards

The final step: celebrate. You've built your self-confidence and your goals are now major milestones, so reward yourself commensurate with your achievements. If your five-year dream involves building an internet business or finishing an Ironman triathlon, treat yourself appropriately when you make your first dollar or finish your first marathon. Reward yourself with a dream vacation, new kitchen cabinets, or whatever matches the size of the milestone. When you reward yourself, rather than someone else rewarding you, you're saying, "*I* did this, and *I* have earned this reward."

That's clear, strong self-confidence: setting major goals, chasing them fearlessly, achieving them, and knowing that you're worth the reward.

Find a Comrade

If you have a close friend or a spouse who's going through a similar process, do so together. If the two of you engage this process in tandem, then you have someone nearby to laugh and learn with, and your chances of increasing your confidence will improve significantly.

You now have a simple but complete model that will help you build your confidence significantly. Don't expect miracles. Changing your consciousness and behavior is hard work that takes months or years. Ups and downs are normal. You might have to cycle through the same process multiple times, giving each step repeated serious attempts until it works.

CHAPTER 3

Relieving Stress

How stressed are you now? And what's bothering you? Is it an assignment due soon? Your detestable boss? Your hillbilly neighbor? Your smirking in-law? Whether your stress arises from your own choices, the people around you, or forces outside your control, relieving it is one of the most important skills you can acquire.

Young or old, rich or poor, novice or expert, civilized or wild—everyone experiences stress (even people who love what they do). A little stress isn't a bad thing, and can it motivate you. High stress, however, is common and damaging. It can harm you physically and ruin your relationships. The good news is that you don't have to experience high stress very often, if you learn how to manage it.

In this chapter, you'll learn about the different ways that stress is created, so you can raise your consciousness and recognize early the circumstances that lead to it. You'll also learn specific and easy-to-use methods to avoid or reduce stress. In the end, it's best to view the amount of stress that you experience like the ancient Stoics did: as the product of your own choices.

What's Bugging You?

Managing your stress involves:

- Identifying the sources of your stress (called stressors). The usual culprits are money issues, job pressures, health concerns, and relationships.

11

- Recognizing any physical symptoms caused by stress, such as fatigue, headache, nausea, and mysterious pains.

- Recognizing any psychological symptoms of stress, such as anger, inordinate nervousness, and crying.

Clearly, elevated stress affects your personal and professional life, perhaps leading to increased tension, fighting with people close to you, and work absences. But it doesn't have to be this way. You can make simple choices to reduce the stress in your life, starting now. Success in managing your stress results from a few small behaviors done correctly over time, and doesn't involve pills, therapy, or platitudes.

To start, you must identify the things that happen to you, whether or not you caused them, that trigger higher levels of stress, anxiety, and tension. The biggest hurdle here is the tendency to avoid thinking about how to deal with stressors. This cycle in particular:

1. Something causes you stress.

2. You stress out for a while, but survive.

3. You choose to not think about the issue.

4. Later, you're forced to deal with the same issue again (return to step 1 and repeat).

That's not stress management—it's coping and denial.

Your goal is to identify your most common handful of stressors. Specifically who, what, where, and when. Answer these questions:

Who's bugging you?
    Usually only one or two individuals are responsible for the most harm, and they're often people who are hard to escape: spouse, parent, child, friend, neighbor, boss, or employee.

What tasks or topics do you dread?
    List the projects, tasks, errands, and subjects of conversation that most make you wince.

Where does it hit you?
    Name the one or two worst physical locations where high stress hits you. Perhaps in your boss's office, at a particular person's house, or in the marital home.

When does it hit you?

During one particular meeting? At a specific time every day? When you get behind the wheel for your commute?

Tip: If you've compiled a long list of work-related tasks in response to the "what" question, then you're probably in the wrong job, and the techniques in this chapter will go only so far in reducing your stress. If you're just not suited to being a wage slave in a hierarchy, consider pursuing a vocation or self-employment instead of just another paycheck.

The who, what, where, and when are vital: knowing your stressors lets you anticipate and manage trigger situations. A short exercise will help. Close your door, turn off your computer and phone, and get some paper. For about five minutes, ponder the last few months of your life and write down the moments when you were most stressed. Be specific about the who, what, where, and when.

Keep this initial list handy, so that you can refine it as you read on. If you actually created the list, rather than just skipping ahead the moment you read "A short exercise will help," then you've likely made a clear mental commitment. The key is admitting that you can't control what those around you say and do, but remembering that you can choose *how* you react.

Tip: Philosophy fans will recognize the admission of noncontrol as the guiding precept of Epictetus's *Enchiridion*.

The tools in this chapter apply mainly to office work, but you can adapt them to other life situations as well. Stress doesn't discriminate. It affects people whether or not they like their work or find it to be meaningful. Upgrading or changing careers may alleviate a bit of anxiety, but it's not a key tool in stress management. Instead, take these three actions while at work: shut people out, cut conversations short, and manage your time. The remaining tools, making sensible choices and starting small, apply in any life situation.

Shut People Out

Control how often you let others interrupt you. This means making yourself scarce (or, politely, managing your accessibility). Let them know through your actions that you're not available universally. The biggest obstacles (by far) are your phone and other pieces of always-on techno-junk. If low stress and productivity are your goals, then you must reclaim significant blocks of your time. By delaying your responses to people, they'll eventually learn that you're not available 24/7.

The solution: disconnect temporarily and selectively. A low-stress day isn't a continual stream of pop-up calendar alerts and new-message chimes. To start, choose a small amount of time, say 30 minutes, to turn off everything that will interrupt you or make noise. Digital withdrawal may induce some finger-drumming agitation at first, but at the end of that 30 minutes, you'll have been more focused and productive than usual and you're likely to feel calmer.

Another way to disconnect is to leave your office building, particularly if your office is one of the "where" entries on your "who, what, where, and when" list.

Where you work is a big part of how you disconnect. Sit outside. Or walk a few blocks to a coffee shop and sit for a few minutes (but avoid carbs, sugar, and stimulants). Bring a meaningful bit of work with you. If it's completely required, tell your boss or a colleague where you're going and when you'll be back. Vary your daily destinations and choose quiet(ish) places that let you focus—libraries, reading rooms, parks, gardens, museums, churches, or hotel lobbies, for example. After an initial bout of disorientation, you'll be surprised how much stress you can avoid by disconnecting. In time, after testing the limits, you'll want to work up to an hour or more each day when you're unreachable.

Tip: If you can't leave the building, you can retreat to an empty conference room or office and shut the door. Or go to the cafeteria during off-hours. (Empty bathroom stalls typically aren't conducive to productivity.)

Cut Conversations Short

For face-to-face interactions, you can choose who to avoid and how to engage someone you can't avoid. Your goal is to reasonably evade people who trigger high-stress reactions. Some interactions are unavoidable, of course, but when possible, sidestep them. You're not trying to ignore or avoid everyone, just the one or two people who truly bug you. Here are some tactics:

- If the irritant will be at a meeting for which you're an inessential invitee, ask your boss if you can skip the meeting and provide the attendees with a short written update so that you can instead work on a more-important task (one that both you and the boss want finished yesterday).

- If the person starts chatting to you in the hall, kitchen, or other common area, resist politely and move on.

- If you see the person in the cafeteria, sit far away.

- If you're invited to lunch and the person will be there, don't go.

These tactics may seem obvious on the page, but when you're actually *in* a situation it's not easy to risk appearing rude in polite society. To say "No," to turn and walk away, to leave abruptly—these are actions that may at first cause you more stress than you're seeking to avoid, but in time you'll realize that most people don't care.

Perhaps you're objecting: "But I can't dodge my boss." Or client. Or employee. Or whoever really stresses you out. In this case, you can still choose *how* to engage. When you must spend time with someone who causes you high stress, interact *only* enough to accomplish the task at hand, then leave. Be respectful and don't be lured into an off-topic side conversation. If another work issue rears its head, don't engage. Cut the conversation short by saying something like, "That's a different conversation, so do we wrap this up? I've got another deadline looming." If personal matters, negative comments about others, gossip, or rumors start to surface, then redirect, be positive, and move on.

But remember that managing stress isn't just about avoiding the negative—it's also about seeking the positive. Connect proactively with people who *improve* your day and lift your spirits—people who make you smile or laugh, people who stimulate your intellect, people who do you favors, people you owe a word of thanks. These connections provide extra resilience in the face of stress.

Seek someone at work with whom you share a personal connection: children in the same school, interest in the same sport or activity, membership in the same community group, or a mutual physical attraction. Such people are often a natural antidote for stress, infecting you with their positive emotions. Even a brief connection by phone, online, or in person can take the edge off and let you to get back to work.

Manage Your Time

For work or life in general, time management—making time work for you instead of against you—is one of the best stress-reducing skills. Chapter 1 covers this topic in detail, but here are a few tips that you can try immediately.

- **Arrive early.** Maybe it's hard for you because you're a late sleeper or you have to chauffeur your kids, but make time to try it. Start by arriving at least 45 minutes early for one day each week. Do so once a week for a month and then reflect on how productive that time was. Note especially what's *missing* from the office: ringing phones, idle chatter, opening and closing doors, and other stress elevators. For most people, the quiet reduces stress, increases focus, and ups productivity.

- **Do the hard stuff first.** Start the day by tackling the most challenging task on your to-do list. Don't start with the easy stuff—knocking out a few trivial tasks doesn't build momentum for tackling a big task. If fact, starting small lures you into doing yet more little tasks to avoid larger, stress-inducing tasks. In the end, this tactic creates *more* stress by delaying what's actually important. Start with the hard stuff and you'll feel better when you're done.

- **Take breaks.** Work about 90 percent of the time and spend the other 10 percent on breaks. For a normal workday, this amounts to two or three breaks of 5–10 minutes each. Experiment to find the optimal work–break balance that maximizes your productivity and minimizes your stress, but keep the work portion under 90 percent—it's not usually true that keeping your head down and working hard all day accomplishes the most work. Walking away from a stressful task lets you cognitively disconnect from it. After a short, positive break, you can return and reconnect, often with higher productivity, sharper focus, and lower stress. Use breaks to do nonwork things: take a walk, call a friend, connect with positive people, or kill some time on the internet.

Tip: You can use a timer or clock app to remind you to break, but it's usually better to break at natural stopping points rather than at arbitrary, fixed times of day.

Choose Wisely

The following practices are well known to reduce stress in life (life in general, not just life at work).

- **Eat well and exercise.** In the vast sea of research here, one of the most important findings to keep in mind is that long-term success at improving your diet and exercise doesn't mean becoming an expert in nutrition or a long-distance swimmer. In this area, taking on mammoth goals too early very often results in relapse. Instead, start small. Choose one or two small diet-and-exercise goals for the year. Stick with simple, measurable goals such as avoiding or reducing one type of food and taking walks a few times each week. Such choices improve your chance of success because they're easier to accomplish and continue practicing in the future.

- **Visualize results.** Every day, spend a few minutes alone quietly visualizing yourself achieving a goal. This technique is popular among athletes, who regularly visualize themselves hitting home runs, sinking putts, or surfing big waves, but you can use it for prosaic tasks as well. Run a detailed movie in your mind of yourself doing what you're trying to achieve. Watch that movie regularly and edit it when necessary to match your current reality. Soon enough, this mental documentary will become a clarifying filter for your daily behaviors, prompting you to ask yourself whether what you're doing will actually help you reach the envisioned outcome. Start with only one goal, and then when you become comfortable in the director's chair, focus on multiple outcomes.

- **Show some gratitude.** Don't let stress trick you into focusing your attention on the negative. At least once each week, stop and inventory the things that you're grateful for because they add value and meaning to your life: family, friends, good looks, sense of humor, status, competence, money, opportunity, health, a roof over your head, or usefulness to others. Contemplating these things regularly fortifies you against high stress levels. Ignore cultural messages about what you're supposed to be grateful for. The full value of gratitude comes from a private, unflinching look at what you're really grateful for, like the failure of a friend or the death of a rival or hated public figure.

- **Pursue contentment.** Do stimulating activities. The answer here depends on your preferences: read a book, ride a bike, learn to play the mandolin, go out with friends, play poker, build a bookcase, or become a volunteer. Choose activities that you know or believe will make you feel content or peaceful. Watching TV isn't stimulating, but writing a screenplay is. Shopping isn't stimulating, but knitting scarves to sell is. Reserve at least 10 percent of every waking day for these activities (no excuses!), and enjoy the results:

  ▸ Positive emotions and personal affirmation

  ▸ A positive identity outside your professional identity

  ▸ Cognitive stimulation focused on areas other than work

  ▸ Become more interesting to others

Start Small

By now, you've probably refined and improved your initial list of stressors, but don't apply what you've learned immediately to address all your stressors. As with diet and exercise, start small by taking comfortable and reasonable steps. Think through the ideas in this chapter and then choose one or two big stressors and one or two specific tactics that you'll commit to trying for a few weeks. Over time, it's normal to find success with some tactics more than others. Your goal is to stay engaged and find the larger handful of tactics that works for you. Life is short—enjoy it as much as civilization permits. And remember the words of Epictetus:

Of things some are in our power, and others are not. In our power are opinion, movement toward a thing, desire, aversion (turning from a thing), and in a word, whatever are our own acts; not in our power are the body, property, reputation, offices (magisterial power), and in a word, whatever are not our own acts.

CHAPTER 4

Engaging in Office Politics

A re you often caught by surprise by the key decisions that your group or your boss makes? Are you often on the losing side of those decisions? And are you often left out of conversations leading up to those decisions? If so, then it's time to discard the idea that workplaces are meritocracies and develop your inner Machiavelli. Virtually every workplace that involves more than a handful of people is an organizational hierarchy, in which people are ranked and rewarded according to status and authority more than ability. Success in such organizations, defined as steady movement toward the leadership ranks, is typically a function of:

- **Likeability.** When you're likeable, people want you involved. If you're not likeable by nature, then become conspicuously more useful to others and learn how to evoke empathy or sympathy. Even sociopaths can and do learn to be liked. In general, only those at or above your level need to like you. Those below you in the hierarchy typically lack the influence to sabotage you.

- **Allies at work.** Allies look out for allies, whether or not the alliance is based on merit, and people tend to develop professional alliances based on a natural fit (outside of work, such people may develop friendships). Despite the maxim, "It's not what you know, it's who you know," abilities tend to trump alliances at the lower and middle levels of a hierarchy, but alliances can be used to reinforce abilities.

- **Significant achievements.** Your education, work skills, and recent work accomplishments give you momentum, which makes your next success more likely because others will tend to view and treat you favorably.

- **Political savvy.** A savvy political operator (or, politely, a strategic thinker) makes new connections regularly, understands coalitions, and makes decisions by using political information. Despite its tarnished reputation, political maneuvering needn't be negative or unethical. Most of the time, it's normal and useful.

If you were educated in the West (the U.S., in particular), you can be forgiven for thinking that resources and rewards are doled out to the deserving. In fact, merit has little to do with it—it's largely people-related work skills and interpersonal dynamics that make or break careers.

Even high-performing workplaces (Wall Street trading floors and Hollywood studios, for example) are only somewhat meritocratic—relationship-based political behaviors affect most outcomes. Success requires not only practical skills and knowledge, but an understanding of interactions of the people around you and the dynamics of decision making. The good news is that you can learn these skills.

Tip: Intelligence (general cognitive ability) is important too, but not enough to get its own bullet point. In general, the higher you rise in the hierarchy, the brighter people tend to be, but with substantial variability. Smart people are a dime a dozen—you're going to need political savvy as well.

Map the Situation

When you make a decision or choose which position to back in a group decision, you must understand the:

- Relevant areas of work (practical and technical knowledge)

- Viability of the options being considered

- Politics of the situation

As a politician animal, suppress the reckless urge to decide or advocate for what *you* feel is correct, no matter how others feel about it. Accurately assessing group politics requires an acute awareness of your own social standing, which limits your latitude in imposing your will on the group when others oppose you. Be cautious and honest in self-assessing your social standing, also called social capital. It's a limited resource that you'll want to seldom spend. If the issue at hand isn't particularly important to you, don't take a hard stand. Save your capital for important issues that offer poor odds.

If the odds are with you in an important situation, you won't have to spend social capital to win. If the odds are against you, you'll have to spend capital by speaking up, deliberating, arguing, posturing, or otherwise influencing others. Assessing odds is more art than science. It begins well before any meeting where big decisions are made. To start, map the key players involved in the decision, their major relationships with the other players, and their likely motives in this situation. If more than two key people are involved, sketch a physical map of influences rather than draw a mental map. Each person will have:

- A place in the formal hierarchy (the organization chart)

- Influence outside formal hierarchical pathways (regardless of the org chart)

- A strong voice in this decision

- Social capital

- Connections to others inside and outside the organization

- Ongoing projects that relate to the current decision

Next, list the likely major outcomes of this decision (often, only two or three outcomes are viable). For each possible outcome, decide who wins and who loses, considering:

- Who's backed who in the past

- Departmental rivalries

- Competing projects

- Limited budgets

Also, account for everyone else's political motivations. Savvy politicians play to win, not to do the right or sensible thing, and will choose the side that they think puts them on a winning path. They might choose a decision because they want to back an ally, because it will hinder or stop someone else's plans, or because it's the most likely to be adopted by the group and put them on the winning team. Strategic thinkers don't view events in isolation. They consider how each decision is connected to other decisions, and the long-term interests of the other people involved.

You can gather intelligence in the usual ways: office gossip, overheard conversations, shoulder surfing, email histories, direct conversations, and so on. Each method has its risks. For example, if you try to feel out key players by initiating conversations with them, some will blab and others will clam up. Either way, you risk being branded as a politician in a negative sense. No matter what insight you may gain prior to the decision-making meeting, you risk being perceived as someone who works angles to gain advantage. That's why it's best to engage in overt political conversation rarely. By not engaging, your aura is that of serious concern about the issue, and others will assign more weight to your words.

Tip: One of my favorite books on this topic is Frank Herbert's *Dune*, a science-fiction novel about the politics of resource scarcity. The maneuverings of each of the novel's many factions (and individuals therein) affect all the other factions, who respond in kind.

Decide

Meeting time. When the time comes to state your decision publicly, you can plead your case for what you want (fight) or let someone else prevail (concede). If the issue isn't important to you, just concede, even if you can win without spending much social capital or stepping on powerful toes. Conceding increases the chance that the winners will later support you when you advocate for something that's important to you.

If the issue is too important for you to concede, and the alternative outcomes weaken you, then instead decide how to best argue your position based on your influence map. The most common strategies are:

- **Bargain.** The exchange of favors for mutual gain goes by many names: logrolling, horse trading, backscratching, and so on. Before the meeting, negotiate candidly with one or more others and agree that if they support you on issue A, you'll support them on issue B. Use this tactic sparingly if possible, lest your work life become a tangle of overlapping and contradictory quid pro quo agreements.

- **Build rapport.** If a person isn't a candidate for horse trading, then instead build rapport by giving them assistance in whatever ways you can. Doing favors signals that you can offer your support on future issues that aren't related to the current one. Make a few deposits in a person's favor bank, and often you'll engender feelings of reciprocity in the recipient.

After Deciding

After you win a decision, try to make amends with the losers in ways that might help you later. You can offer bits of your budget, allocate resources, lend personnel, offer votes on upcoming decisions, and so on. And if *you* lose, note whether the winners attempt to build bridges with you and any others who didn't get their way.

Consider how your place in the hierarchy will shift over time as coalitions form and dissolve, and as power ebbs and flows. One of the most difficult lessons to accept in a charged political atmosphere is that it's not all about us versus them or who's right versus who's wrong.

Play the Long Game

For continued success, you must remain aware of the current state of politics in your group and your organization. Any political behaviors must be tempered by workplace norms. Some organizations require a subtle political touch, whereas others foster robust maneuvering.

Tip: Some organizations claim to shun politics entirely. In my two decades of consulting for firms of all sizes, I've never come across a place where this claim held true, and I suspect that it holds nowhere outside of egalitarian hunter-gatherer tribes.

If you're a newcomer or a beginner, start by choosing one upcoming significant decision, issue, or project where you'll be one of the key players. Draw the influence map, apply the preceding techniques, and estimate your odds of success. Decide whether bargaining or rapport-building with the other players is appropriate. Consider how you'll improve relationships with the losers, should you win.

Ignoring office politics leaves you out of the loop and stalls your rise in the hierarchy. Obsessing over them for every decision, on the other hand, distracts you from your real work and will likely cast you in a bad light. Your goal is to engage in politics in such a way that you give yourself a fighting chance on the issues that matter most. To get attention and respect from the strongest players at work, show that you understand and value long-term, strategic political thinking.

CHAPTER 5

Negotiating and Achieving Mutual Benefits

Anegotiation is, simply, a conversation that leads to an agreement. But many of us come to the bargaining table believing that negotiation is a contentious and stressful attempt to convince our bargaining partner to do something that they don't want to do. There's a better way. This chapter will teach you the methods that skilled communicators use to achieve mutual benefits at the negotiation table.

Preparing to Negotiate

To be a successful negotiator, show up prepared. You can work off-the-cuff in minor negotiations, but proper preparation gives you the information and confidence to think on your feet, tap your creativity, and be at ease during the conversation. To prepare, work through the following six steps to give yourself a solid footing and set the stage for a successful negotiation. Spend the time up front, and it will pay off in the end. The examples in this chapter focus on career and salary negotiations, but the same or similar steps apply to solving a problem with a neighbor or a friend, networking and creating business partnerships, or making major purchases such as a house or car.

1. **Research** is by far the most important step, so don't skip it thinking that you can rely on your wit and charm to wing it. For this example, determine what your market value is. Resources like *salary.com*,

glassdoor.com, and *getraised.com*, as well as government websites, provide salary data based on job title, education, years experience, and geographic region. During your research, ask yourself:

If you're an employee, are you asking for raises and increased benefits on a yearly basis?

If you're an employee, what projects did you contribute to that increased your employer's profits?

If you're a consultant or entrepreneur, are you pricing your services based on what the market is willing to pay for them?

If you're a consultant or entrepreneur, can the market that you're now serving afford to pay what your services are worth?

After determining what your services are worth, decide what your requirements are and what you'll do if they're not met. This course of action is called your BATNA, or the Best Alternative To a Negotiated Agreement. Ask yourself, "What is the least I will accept and still be happy?"

Next, be ready to sing your own praises. List your significant skills and their corresponding results that are relevant to your upcoming negotiation. Here's a sample list:

Skill → Result
Communication → Increased revenue
Research → Developed policy framework
Strategic planning → Expanded operation

2. **Prioritize** and list all the vital points of your negotiation. For job seekers, the vital points are salary, bonuses, stock options, job title, vacation time, and health benefits, and possibly flextime, telecommuting, maternity or paternity leave, and take-home vehicle.

3. Map the **concessions** that you're willing to make. For anything that you give up, you're going to ask for something in exchange (reciprocity). If you skip this step, then you'll become a doormat during the negotiation. Would you take a higher starting salary in exchange for a lower bonus? Are you willing to forgo a few vacation days in exchange for more flextime?

4. Learn as much as you can about the **needs** of your bargaining partner. Conduct a web search (using Google, Bing, Archive.org, and so on) for the other party. Investigate your bargaining partner's website and social media presence—they're doing the same to find out about you. What do they say about themselves? What do others say about them? Learn what your bargaining partner wants to accomplish, then prepare to talk about how your skills, results, and accomplishments can help them reach their goals.

5. Determine your common **connections** inside and outside the organization. Most likely you'll be finding ways to name-drop at strategic points in your negotiation. Make sure that your connections are credible.

6. Learn who the **stakeholders** and decision makers are. When you're interviewing for a job, you might be starting with the Human Resources department, or you might be interviewed by the team you'll be working with. You should understand the decision-making process in advance.

Researching Careers and Salaries

Your values and priorities should inform your search for the right compensation, so do some hands-on work:

- Research the market

- Price your goods, services, salary, and benefits accordingly

- Recognize opportunities to negotiate compensation for time, services, or products

- Ask for what you want based on the value that you bring rather than what you need to make ends meet or what you think is fair

Your market value isn't about just covering your expenses—it's about taking your long-term priorities and goals in your life and work into account. To get started, make a few lists:

1. List the services you provide or products you sell and indicate what you're currently charging for them.

2. List the benefits that your clients, customers, or employers derive from your work.

3. Based on the preceding two lists, list all the people and businesses that might use your services or buy your products, focusing on the high end. The four column headings for this list should be Services Provided, Cost, Benefits, and People/Businesses.

4. Categorize your work. Using the Bureau of Labor Statistics National Wage Data website (*www.bls.gov/oes/current/oes_stru.htm*), find as many job or service categories that apply to your work and rank them from highest to lowest average wage. Note where your current position ranks and bump yourself up a level. Be flexible with regard to your occupational title. If you're a nurse, teacher, or manager, for example, might you also be a health care manager, trainer, or executive, respectively?

5. List the most respected, accomplished, high-earning people in your field or similar fields. Contact at least three of these people to find out how much they earn or charge. Alternatively, post a question on LinkedIn, Facebook, or any relevant forum or social networking website.

Use web resources to research the market value of your skills. The following sites, for example, contain industry and often employer-specific information on salary and benefits by job category.

- *salary.com*

- *glassdoor.com*

- *getraised.com*

- *vault.com*

- *payscale.com*

- Compare what you now do to jobs paying six-figure incomes:

  swz.salary.com/salarywizard/layouthtmls/swzl_salaryrangenarrow_50.html

- Find out where you stand in terms of salary in your industry:

  my.monster.com/Career-Assessment/Dashboard.aspx

- Occupational Employment Statistics, including national wage data:

  www.bls.gov/oes/current/oes_stru.htm

- Salary and wage information from the U.S. Department of Labor: *www.careeronestop.org/SalariesBenefits/Sal_default.aspx*

Getting the Most Out of This Chapter

As with any worthwhile skill, you'll be much more successful if you practice what you learn in your daily life. Before you continue, reflect on your daily experience to notice your opportunities to negotiate. Ask yourself:

What have you been negotiating repeatedly with little or no success?

Who or what gets in your way?

What did you have the opportunity to negotiate today? For example, did anyone ask you to do something for them? Did you offer your help or services to another? What did you pay for today?

Distributive Bargaining and Interest-Based Bargaining

Is effective negotiation about getting what you want? Or is it about everyone getting what they want? Two major strategies will help you answer these questions:

- **Distributive bargaining** divides a limited number of benefits or resources. Suppose that you have six pieces of pie. Your job would be to get more slices than your bargaining partner. Used as your sole strategy, distributive bargaining is a win–lose proposition. Somebody gets more, while the other gets less.

- **Interest-based bargaining** (also called **mutual-benefit negotiation**) is about discovering your bargaining partner's interests, needs, and preferences. The goal of this strategy is to expand the pie of benefits, attempting to satisfy as many mutual interests as possible.

These two strategies are often illustrated with a story about two little sisters arguing about who gets the last orange. Their mom, a skilled problem solver, asks her daughters what they want to do with the orange (instead of just cutting the orange in half and walking away). One daughter explains that she wants to eat it, whereas the other daughter reveals that she wants to make zest for her cupcakes. The mother's questions are key to uncovering each daughter's wishes. She stops the argument and satisfies both girls. Notice that both strategies are used. The mother asks questions that help reveal both daughters' interests (interest-based bargaining) and then she distributes the orange according to their preferences (distributive bargaining).

Most negotiations become distributive at some point, after you've brainstormed and expanded the pie, you will eventually need to distribute the resources. In most cases, you'll produce better outcomes by using both strategies.

Diagnostic Questions

At the heart of interest-based bargaining is a technique called diagnostic questioning. Asking diagnostic questions will help you figure out what your bargaining partners' interests are or what they want out of the deal. Diagnostic questions are open-ended, usually starting with words like who, what, when, where, why, and how, or phrases like, "Tell me more about...".

Diagnostic questions are also used to expand a conversation. Asking your boss a closed-ended question like, "Do you think it's possible for me to get a raise this year?" gives your boss the chance to answer with a simple, "No." Instead, use open-ended questions. Start the conversation with questions like, "How is the restructuring going for you personally?" or, "What do you like about working in the new building?" Asking open-ended questions sets the tone and engages in issues that matter to both you and your bargaining partner. After you've established this connection, start the negotiation. Ask a question like, "What results do you most want to see me produce to justify a raise next year?" This question shows that you're aligning yourself with company expectations and are a team player willing to benefit the entire organization. Your boss will likely see that you want to accomplish group goals and are not purely self-interested.

Open-ended questions are most effective when you run into objections or flat-out refusal. They let you dig a little deeper and create an atmosphere of mutual problem solving. In the absence of facts and information, we tend to mind read and make assumptions, or worse, we try to convince people to do something they don't want to do. Asking diagnostic questions helps you gain clarity and guide the conversation toward agreement.

Sample Diagnostic Questions

To help you master this technique, use the following list of sample diagnostic questions as a cheat sheet. If you get stuck, remember: who, what, when, where, why, and how.

Salary questions

What issues might bear on my salary increase this year?

Who besides _____ might influence the company's decision on the size of my raise?

Who do you need to satisfy to close a deal? How can I help you satisfy them?

Who has the authority to close the deal? Should we include them in our discussions?

What should I be prepared to demonstrate about my performance to maximize my raise this year?

What limitations might you be operating under that I'm unaware of?

How can I help remove or diminish those limitations?

What are your primary goals for the coming year?

How might I help you achieve them?

What metrics do you base the company's proposed raise this year?

If I were to accept your counteroffer, what could you promise me as a timeline for getting to X salary?

What would it take to adjust my salary at target points as opposed to annual reviews?

Can you think of any items within the scope of this discussion that are of low cost to you but might be of high value to me?

Would you be willing to brainstorm other ideas and options?

Deal and fee-setting questions

What are your financial goals for the year?

What were your goals for last year and did you meet them?

What obstacles prevented you from being as successful as you wished to be last year?

If you could eliminate or reduce some of those obstacles, what would it be worth to you?

What have you budgeted this year for services like mine?

What did you base that budget on?

What other items have you budgeted as little/as much on?

In what ways do you anticipate spending the money that you budgeted for services like mine?

Are you currently paying for services like mine?

Have those services lived up to your expectations?

When you hire a _____, what are your preferences in the manner the job is done?

What do you demand by way of quality?

How might we pass the expense of _____ along to the customer?

What other sources of income or another budget item could be used to pay for my services?

Would you be willing to give me a chance to show you a better way to do X?

If I could produce X results, would you be comfortable entering into a contingency deal, a flat fee with a bonus, or an hourly rate with a bonus?

Is there something of value that you believe you could provide to me in addition to cash that might incentivize me to do the job for less than my going rate?

Issue-oriented questions

How would you characterize the issue/problem?

Who do we need to include in the conversation?

Who might be harmed as a result of this issue?

How can I help you avoid that harm?

Where do you think we might get more information that would help us resolve this problem?

Would you like me to search for that information?

What's most important to you?

What's least important to you?

What would be the best outcome for you?

What's difficult about X?

How can I help you?

How do you see our relationship evolving if we resolve this issue?

What do you fear might happen if we don't resolve it?

What's holding you back?

Where do you wish you could go?

What would you do if your hands weren't tied?

If we were partners in this, how could we use our strengths to support each other?

What role would you like me to play in resolving some of the problems you're having with X now?

What's upsetting you?

What do you think is fair?

Why do you think that's fair?

What about that resolution seems fair?

What else?

What might be left unsaid or undone?

Conflict Resolution

Sometimes we enter into a negotiation feeling like we're at a disadvantage. Our bargaining partner may want more than we can give, or we fear that what we ask for might be rejected out of hand. These negotiations are especially tough if our bargaining partner perceives all negotiation as conflict rather than conversation. Consequently, we develop strategies, such as subconscious styles or ingrained responses, for easing our fear.

Unfortunately, these strategies can hinder our ability to produce the desired outcome in negotiation. The main strategies for dealing with conflict are:

- **Avoidance.** You've had an argument with a friend or a coworker, so you avoid their calls or emails for days before trying to resolve the matter.

- **Suppression.** Somebody asks you for a favor or to talk about a sticky subject, and you flat-out refuse.

- **Resolution.** You acknowledge the problem or the issue, and you offer to make things right.

- **Transformation.** You use the conflict to change your behavior with the goal of transforming not just the conflict, but the relationship as well.

- **Transcendence.** You move past the need to engage in the conflict in the first place. That is, the conflict no longer triggers a knee-jerk reaction.

Avoidance and suppression are the most common (and typically least productive) strategies. Resolution is a bit more conscious and evolved. Transformation and transcendence are practiced by mature, skilled negotiators.

To become a better negotiator, turn up your self-awareness. Be honest with yourself and see how you typically respond to conflict, and then turn your observations into action by challenging yourself to resolve a conflict. Over the next few days, pay attention to your typical reactions to conflict in your relationships at home and work.

Contentious Tactics

When you decide that you want or need something, and you pursue it, you put yourself in the path of potential conflict with someone or something.

Not everyone you deal with will know how to engage in problem solving by asking diagnostic questions or brainstorming to expand the conversation. Instead, your bargaining partner may resort to contentious tactics to try to hold their ground or keep as many of the pieces of the pie as possible.

Learn to recognize these tactics, so you can either disengage, meet fire with fire, or change the game. The most common contentious tactics are all attempts to manipulate a bargaining partner. They are:

- **Ingratiation.** Getting what one wants through charm or flattery or being likeable. This tactic is useful and most appreciated when it's authentic. "Hey, you're really a better editor than I am. Would you take a look at this document?"

- **Promises.** Getting what one wants now by agreeing to do something later. This tactic is most useful when used for mutual gain, rather than as a power play. "I'll deliver X to you on an expedited basis, but only if you pay me my normal charge up front and a bonus at the time of delivery."

- **Shaming.** Expressions of dismay, shock, or disapproval of another's behavior, usually on moral grounds. This tactic is much more common than is usually admitted, and it can destroy relationships. "Your work is embarrassing and you're not living up to your potential."

- **Persuasive argumentation.** The use of logic and reason to change somebody's behavior or position. This tactic is often used to prove that the other party is wrong or to lower the other party's expectations.

When you observe one of these tactics in action, do you disengage, meet fire with fire, or change the game? If you're in harm's way, disengage. For all other situations, remember that every threat and accusation is a plea for help. Here are a few ways to navigate contentious tactics:

- **Focus on the problem, not the person.** Avoid blame and insults. Shifting the focus is also a sign of your skill and value.

- **Reflect what you hear.** Be an active listener. Paraphrase what's been said but let your bargaining partner know the effect of their words. Use diagnostic questions and brainstorm to help return to cooperation.

- **Name the problem.** After reflecting your bargaining partner's opinion or perspective, identify the underlying issue. Doing so often defuses the tension and brings people back to cooperation.

Most contentious tactics are not inherently good or bad; they're survival tools that people have been using since the dawn of spoken language. By recognizing them as they're happening, you'll be better prepared to pause, slow things down, and depersonalize the situation. Then you can make collaborative choices in the moment.

Some (bad) contentious tactics that you may also experience are:

- **Gamesmanship.** Getting what one wants by pushing the rules or ratcheting up the stakes, like forcing a foul in basketball. The sole purpose of this tactic is to come out ahead. "If I have to give you ten days notice, I'll give it to you at 5 P.M. on Christmas Eve."

- **Threats.** Getting what one wants by threatening to cause the other harm if they don't comply. Threats can vary from subtle to frightening and be delivered via any communications channel (email, face-to-face, the rumor mill, and so on). "If you don't submit your report, you're going to have to work over the weekend."

- **Physical force (violence).** Hitting, pushing, shoving, taking.

Opening the Negotiation

You've done your research, you know what you want, and you know your market value. You're now prepared to sit down with your bargaining partner. To start a solid negotiation:

- **Establish a connection with your bargaining partner.** Establishing connection and trust is mainly a matter of small talk. People often make the mistake of cutting to the chase in an effort to appear businesslike and time-conscious. But research shows that breaking the ice by talking about kids or cars or new offices releases the feel-good bonding hormone oxytocin. Research also shows that negotiations taking place over coffee or a meal produce much more favorable outcomes. Don't underestimate the power of small talk and breaking bread.

- **Engage in active listening.** Let your bargaining partner know that you understand their perspectives and issues. This technique involves paraphrasing key points throughout the conversation. When using active listening skills, you're learning what's working or not working for your bargaining partner, so paraphrase what you hear and continue to ask diagnostic questions. You're attempting to expand that pie of possibilities and gather as much information as possible to dovetail your offer with their needs.

- **Frame your opening requests as a benefit.** After you've established a connection and listened to your bargaining partner, frame your opening offer or request. Position it as a benefit to them to let them know how you can help them solve a problem or fill an expressed need. Address every issue and goal by explaining how your services or skills will help them accomplish those goals.

Framing

Framing creates perspective. If you're negotiating with a potential client, and you learn how dissatisfied they were with a former consultant for missing project deadlines, then you can frame your services in a new light. Tell them how you've come in under budget or ahead of schedule, offer to put them in touch with clients for whom you've done similar work, and finish by offering a starting fee for the project. This approach frames your request around time, budget, and reputation as benefits to your bargaining partner, and anchors the price.

In general, framing:

- Focuses attention

- Influences judgments

- Organizes a person's thoughts around a specific category or outcome

- Creates responses that people tend to use to fit the frame

A question as innocuous as, "How tall is he?" frames that response in terms of height. Research shows that people give higher numbers when asked how tall or large someone is than they do when asked how short or small someone is.

Many negotiations look and sound like contests between right and wrong. It's critical that you learn to frame and reframe the subject to converse in a way that encourages people to move from competition to collaboration. Here are some ways to reframe negotiations that are going poorly:

- When a conversation becomes adversarial, shift the focus from the negotiators to the problem. That is, be hard on the problem and soft on the people.

- If you or your bargaining partner are stuck on being right, acknowledge that you're on opposite sides and use diagnostic questions to shift the focus and find out what they really want.

- If you're willing to make concessions but your bargaining partner is not, reframe the situation by changing the emphasis from the roadblock to exploring other possibilities.

- When somebody is stuck in the past, encourage them to look forward to the next steps. Remind them what's done is done, and the solution lies in what's ahead.

Framing Examples and Exercises

To counter resistance, rejection, or limited thinking, try reframing by using the following examples as a guide.

Example 1:

Frame: "It's not personal. Nobody's getting raises."

Reframe: "I've been doing the work of three positions and producing great results for the company, and I'd like to talk about bringing my salary and title into alignment with the reality of what amounts to a new job description."

Example #2:

Frame: "As a professional business association, we don't pay our monthly speakers; people are happy to speak for free for the marketing possibilities."

Reframe: "As a professional, I make part of my living by speaking. Perhaps we can brainstorm ways to underwrite my talk without impacting your budget or your policy."

Now, reframe the following statements to turn the conversation around.

"I can't raise my fees, nobody will hire me."

"The sales department keeps promising numbers that production can't make."

"If I support your work on this new project, I'm going to lose you to another department."

"Your resume indicates you don't remain long in any given position."

"Your hourly rate is too high."

Anchoring

Anchoring establishes a reference point around which a negotiation will revolve. Whoever makes the first reasonable offer sets the anchor, and the remainder of the negotiation will revolve around it. For example, listing your house for $425,900 instead of a round number like $426,000 influences the buyer to make counteroffers in smaller increments. In any negotiation, always try to anchor first and in your favor. If you're a seller, then anchor with a higher price; if you're a buyer, then anchor low.

Anything you're negotiating has positive and negative attributes, or qualities that suggest a higher or lower value. So high anchors direct a person's attention toward an item's positive attributes, whereas low anchors direct attention to its flaws.

If you're buying a used car, for example, you'll likely point out features like high mileage or worn upholstery. As the seller, you might focus on frequent preventative maintenance and highway miles. Making the first offer is crucial, and when your offer is credible and specific, your bargaining partner will typically adjust very little from the anchor.

Another benefit of making an aggressive first offer is that you'll be able to encourage more concessions from your bargaining partner. Suppose that you offer $15000 for a car that lists for $20000, then the dealer counters with $19000. You might be willing to adjust upwards if the dealer sweetens the deal with, say, a couple of features you want or a lower financing rate. In fact, one of the best predictors of negotiation satisfaction is the number and size of concessions that your bargaining partner makes in your favor.

Anchors can also be used against you. If you think that an offer, counteroffer, or concession might cause the conversation to break down, ask diagnostic questions to gain clarity and test the strength of your bargaining partner's position. Then paraphrase your new understanding and assure them that you're confident you can come to an agreement.

Making Range Offers

In some cases, your best strategy for negotiating might be a bolstering range offer, which involves starting at your desired target price and then going up to a reasonable maximum. Findings (*www8.gsb.columbia.edu/ newsroom/newsn/3497*) suggest that bolstering range offers get better overall deals, without being seen any more negatively than other styles. The examples in the accompanying figure consider possible proposals that

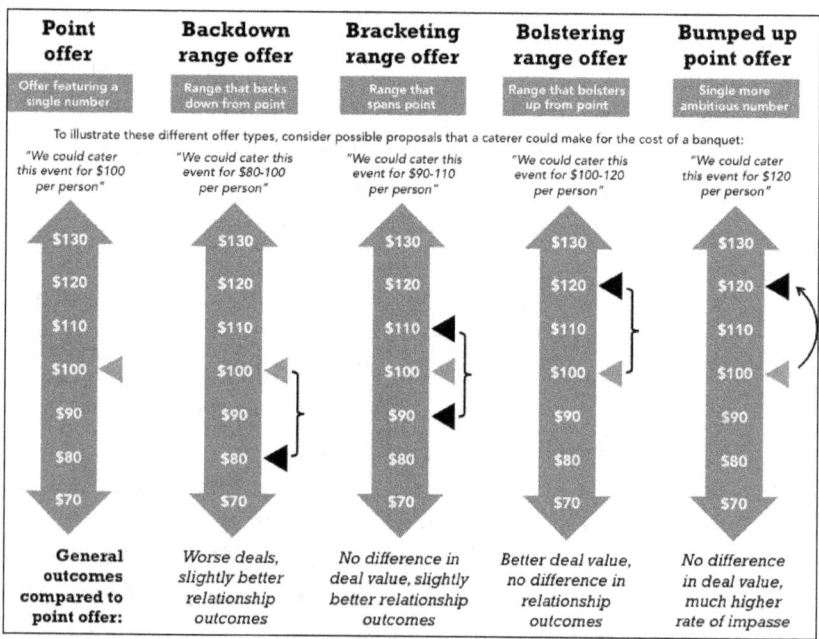

From "Tandem anchoring: informational and politeness effects of range offers in social exchange" (D. Ames and M. Mason, J Pers Soc Psychol. Feb, 2015).

a caterer could make for the cost of a banquet. The point (target) is $100 for providing the service.

Concessions and Reciprocity

A concession is giving away a privilege, a fact, or a piece of your pie, and reciprocity is asking for something in return. Because making concessions and asking for reciprocity is for many people the hardest part of negotiating, it's something that you never want to improvise under pressure. Plan what you're willing to give up and what you might want in return. Without reciprocity, a concession is a one-way transaction, or settling and caving into demands. The result is a whittling away of your interests, preferences, and (sometimes) principles.

If you're entering a career negotiation, for example, then you must know your priorities before you even start talking. Is it a deal breaker if you don't get three weeks of vacation every year, or would you be happy with ten days? Do you require two days of telecommuting per week, or would you settle for twice a month?

Here are some key points to help you at the bargaining table:

- When you ask for a concession, listen carefully to your bargaining partner's response and paraphrase what they've said. Follow that up by stressing the fairness of your proposal.

- If your bargaining partner asks you for something in return, stress your willingness to be agreeable while also letting them know how difficult or generous it is.

- If you get stuck or the negotiation stalls, ask diagnostic questions to uncover the underlying reasons and get things moving again.

- If your requests continue to be met with refusal, then suggest pausing to sleep on it, or end the negotiation and walk away. Your bargaining partner will sometimes capitulate in that moment or after thinking about it overnight.

Making concessions and asking for reciprocity requires being creative with the vital points of the negotiation. The goal of negotiation isn't to compromise, but to exchange things of value in a way that satisfies everybody. Of course, *not* coming to an agreement can be a good thing if you're going to regret the outcome.

Uncooperative Bargaining Partners

In a perfect negotiation, your bargaining partner is as invested in your interests as you are in theirs. In reality, you may often deal with people who are argumentative, try to win at all costs, and enjoy crushing their opponent.

Tactics for dealing with an uncooperative bargaining partner are:

- If you sense in advance that you'll be entering a hardball negotiation, craft a side deal first. Do your research and come to the table with options. Having a backup plan can give you a real advantage. If you're a consultant and you've just landed a contract at your top hourly rate, for example, use that agreement to position yourself at the top of the bargaining range with your next client.

- Do your best to match your bargaining partner's conversational style. Take notice as you settle into the conversation. Is your bargaining partner relying on story? On technical information or statistics? On cultural values? In any case, match style for style.

- If you feel at a loss, acknowledge aloud that you might be talking past one another and ask how you might get on the same page.

- If you're stonewalled, meet fire with fire. Consider setting aside the conversation and coming back to it later.

- Be willing to outwait your bargaining partner—the most powerful negotiation tactic is silence.

Next Steps

As you've made your way through this chapter, you've probably noticed several areas of your life and work where you need to negotiate. Start with the low-hanging fruit. Tackle the easy things first to get a feel for the process and create a string of successes. As you move on to higher-stakes negotiations, remember that negotiation is like any art or sport. Practice, rehearse, and always return to the basics. An effective negotiation isn't just a set of applied tools and tactics. It's a commitment to a principle that steers you toward collaboration.

If you're preparing for your next performance review, show your measurable results and network with those who can influence your career. Remember to anchor first, frame your offer, and exchange things of value. If you meet resistance, ask diagnostic questions. And never forget, the most powerful negotiation strategy is silence.

Negotiation Cheat Sheet

1. Research and prepare

2. Prioritize your vital points

3. Map your concessions

4. Know your bottom line

5. Convene the decision makers or stakeholders

6. Establish connection and trust (small talk)

7. Ask open-ended questions

8. Anchor first and anchor high

9. Frame your request as a benefit to your bargaining partner

10. Meet an impasse or "No" with brainstorming

11. Name concessions and ask for reciprocity

12. Paraphrase your understanding

13. Reach agreement and write it down

Terms and Definitions

Anchoring
    Establishing a reference point (anchor) around which a negotiation will revolve. Anchoring creates a favorable bargaining range for the first party who makes a reasonable offer. The anchor will influence the other party's responses in the direction of the anchor throughout the negotiation.

Concessions

Conceding, yielding, or exchanging things of value for relatively little or nothing in return.

Contentious tactics

Attempts to convince your bargaining partner to do something she doesn't want to do or to stop doing something she wants to continue doing. Tactics include ingratiation, promises, shaming, persuasive argumentation, gamesmanship, threats, and physical force.

Diagnostic questions

Open-ended questions that start with words like who, what, when, where, why, and how. Used to discover the interests of your bargaining partner to find mutual benefit, and to help you move past objections or an impasse.

Distributive bargaining

Attempting to distribute among parties what they perceive to be limited resources. The subject of the negotiation is viewed as a "fixed pie" and the goal is to get as many slices as possible.

Framing

Creating a perspective of the problems or issues for a decision. If you can frame the points of negotiation as benefits to your bargaining partner, you are poised to achieve a favorable outcome for both parties.

Interest-based bargaining (mutual-benefit negotiation)

Entering into a value-expanding conversation by first identifying all parties' interests and then trying to satisfy all interests.

Interests

All parties' needs, desires, fears, motives, preferences, priorities, appetites for risk, and predictions about the future.

Negotiation

Discussions between at least two parties for the purpose of reaching an agreement. A negotiation can entail trying to get someone to do something they don't want to do; trying to get someone to stop doing something they want to continue to do; or trying to satisfy everyone's interests in the points of the negotiation.

Reciprocity
The practice of exchanging things with others for mutual benefit.

Further Reading

27 Powers of Persuasion: Simple Strategies to Seduce Audiences & Win Allies by Chris St. Hilaire

3D Negotiations: Powerful Tools to Change the Game in Your Most Important Deals by David A. Lax and James K. Sebenius

Ask For It: How Women Can Use the Power of Negotiation to Get What They Really Want by Linda Babcock and Sara Laschever

Brain Rules: 12 Principles for Surviving and Thriving at Work, Home, and School by John Medina

Drive: The Surprising Truth About What Motivates Us by Daniel H. Pink

Getting Past No by William Ury

Getting to Yes: Negotiating Agreement Without Giving In by Roger Fisher

Influence: The Psychology of Persuasion by Robert B. Cialdini

Leadership Presence by Kathy Lubar and Belle Linda Halpern

Leadership and Self-Deception: Getting Out of the Box by The Arbinger Institute

Negotiation Genius: How to Overcome Obstacles and Achieve Brilliant Results at the Bargaining Table and Beyond by Deepak Malhotra and Max Bazerman

No Excuses: 9 Ways Women Can Change How We Think About Power by Gloria Feldt

The Mind and Heart of the Negotiator by Leigh Thompson

Women Don't Ask: The High Cost of Avoiding Negotiation—and Positive Strategies for Change by Linda Babcock and Sara Laschever

CHAPTER 6

Overcoming Procrastination

By kicking your procrastination habit, you can wring more productivity out of your day without working any longer or any harder. Procrastinators feel that they sacrifice quality because of a time crunch, and develop a sense of panic when they put things off a little too long. Procrastination is a habit worth kicking. People who procrastinate may feel guilty, and they're likely to experience more colds, aches, stress, and insomnia than nonprocrastinators.

Are You a Procrastinator?

Two common behaviors appear to be procrastination on the surface but aren't:

- **Prioritizing.** In a hectic work day, suppose that your to-do list has 50 items. If you prioritize that list and then do the first 25 tasks in priority order, leaving 25 unfinished tasks at the end of the day, then that's not procrastinating. It's prioritizing, which is a healthy time-management skill.

- **Delaying with reason.** Delaying action on purpose isn't procrastination. Suppose that you have a big decision to make, but you haven't quite collected all the necessary data. That's a wise time to put off taking action. Or imagine that you have a big project, and you've got a couple of months to finish it. It's almost time to start the project,

49

but if you wait another day or two, you'll have a new computer, or new software, or more people to help you. Putting it off may actually save you time in the long run, so it's wise to delay action.

Think about your procrastination habit. Is it true procrastination? Or are you actually prioritizing or delaying action for a good reason?

True procrastination is putting off a priority task or project without reason. You need to get it done. You want to get it done. But for some reason you just keep putting it off. *That's* procrastination—your biggest, time-sapping, productivity-killing, time-management challenge.

What You Put Off

Get a pen and paper and list the things that you tend to put off. A written list can offer concrete insights into your procrastination habit.

My own list (I was a procrastinator too) looked like this:

What do I put off?

▶ Writing reports

▶ Returning emails

▶ Sending thank-you notes

▶ Sending holiday cards

I realized quickly that I was putting off anything related to writing.

If you get stuck creating your list, you may find it helpful to instead list things that you *never* put off. What tasks are you jumping on every day? When you're done, compare the items on your list. It may help you to start understanding your procrastination habit.

How You Procrastinate

Procrastination has warning signs. Don't fall for your own excuses. You're in danger of procrastinating when you hear yourself thinking things like:

"I have plenty of time to get to that project."

"I work better under pressure."

"I'll get to it, but first I just want to..."

Certain behaviors are also red flags that you're about to procrastinate. When I was a fellow procrastinator, I had my favorite stalling tactics. I would sit down to do a writing project and feel the dread creeping in. Suddenly, I had a deep urge to do something else:

How do I stall?

▶ Sharpen my pencils

▶ Make a cup of coffee

▶ Check my email

▶ Browse work-related websites

Most of these behaviors gave me the illusion of being productive, but I was really just stalling.

And you? What are your favorite stalling tactics? What excuses and behaviors do you allow yourself to avoid doing your priority project? You started a list earlier that had *what* you tend to procrastinate about. Go back to those notes and add your list of *how* you stall.

Why You Procrastinate

Now that you've listed the what and how of your procrastinating, let's look at the why. People tend to procrastinate for five main reasons:

• You lack confidence. You want to do a good job, but you're just not sure that you know how.

• You're easily distracted. Oops, you forgot it again.

• You're overwhelmed. A monstrous job looms over you, and you don't know where to start.

• You're creatively blocked. You want to have a brilliant idea, yet you have nothing.

• You dread it. You hate the task.

Add the reasons that resonate with you to your procrastination profile, listed under *Why do I procrastinate?* The following sections cover each reason in more detail and describe strategies to help you overcome your procrastination habit.

You Lack Confidence

You're not sure that you know how to do a good job. Try the following strategies:

- **Build your skills.** When people compare the list of what they always avoid with the list of what they never avoid, they often realize that they're avoiding tasks because they lack confidence or skill in the "always avoid" areas. In my own case of putting off everything related to writing, I realized that every time I sat down to write a document, a voice in my head said, "You're a terrible writer. If you finish and distribute this document, then everyone will know it." I was procrastinating because I lacked the confidence and skill to write, so I took writing and editing classes.

- **Replace negative thoughts with positive ones.** Even though I improved my writing, I still couldn't sit down to write without hearing my inner voice saying, "You're a terrible writer." Eventually, I realized that I needed to replace the old mental message with a new one. I had to learn to say, "I've got new skills, and writing this report is an opportunity for me to practice those skills" and "I may not be a perfect writer, but everyone makes some mistakes."

- **Set realistic standards.** As a procrastinator, you probably tend to set unrealistically high expectations for yourself. If so, re-examine those standards. Your mantra should be production before perfection.

- **Visualize your success.** In the end, I found it helpful when I was writing to visualize how relieved I was going to feel when the project was done. Perhaps you're focusing on each step of the process, causing you to spin your wheels and feel even more afraid of the task. Instead, visualize your successful completion.

You're Easily Distracted

There's always some distraction that makes you stray off course. Try the following strategies:

- **Improve your personal working environment.** Clear all the clutter off your desk. Close your door, or orientate your body so that your back is to the flow of traffic. Or pick up the whole project and move somewhere with fewer distractions.

- **Use distractions as rewards.** If you love to check your email or browse the web, then allow yourself to do so only after you work for a fixed duration (say, 30 minutes) or complete a mini-milestone (say, three pages of the writing). With a little discipline, you can use the very distractions that tend to make you procrastinate as rewards for accomplishing the task that you're avoiding.

- **Cut the chatter.** Stay on course; socialize later. If a friend stops by wanting to chat about the weekend, say, "I need to work on this project for just 30 minutes, then I'll come find you."

You're Overwhelmed

You're paralyzed into inactivity because a monstrous task is barreling at you. Try the following strategies:

- **Break down the project into manageable tasks.** If you divide a big project into a hundred bite-sized steps, then you can work through it step-by-step until finally the whole project is behind you. This strategy also gives you some control because you can choose which steps to work on each day.

- **Set interim deadlines.** Find an accountability partner (a colleague or your boss) and promise to turn in certain parts of work on your project, leading up to your ultimate deadline. In a related business-school experiment, researchers divided subjects into three different groups. All were asked to proofread a document and were paid per error found, with penalties for every day late that they submitted their work (after three weeks). The group that had fixed weekly interim deadlines found far more errors and turned in their work far earlier than the groups that had a single deadline (three weeks out) or set their own interim deadlines.

You're Creatively Blocked

You're sick of the work hanging over you and want to get it done, but you're out of ideas. Try the following strategies:

- **Change your location or method.** Have you been in your office all afternoon? Take a walk. Have you been working at your computer? Use pen and paper or a white board.

- **Brainstorm with others.** If you're working alone, run your ideas by a friend or muse to see whether that sparks your creativity.

- **Lower your standards.** You needn't come up with a brilliant idea when it's enough just to get the job done. Remember, production before perfection.

You Dread the Task

You hate the task that's in front of you. You know that it needs to get done, but you just don't want to do it. Try the following strategies:

- **Reward yourself.** If you finish a little bit of the task, give yourself a little reward (a prize or treat). For completing bigger chunks, reward yourself proportionally. You get not only the reward but the satisfaction that part or all of the job is done.

- **Commit ten minutes.** Promise yourself to work on the task for at least ten minutes. Set a timer and, when it beeps, you're done. But first ask yourself whether you still truly hate the task now that the ball is rolling. Often, the work won't feel quite so bad, and you can just keep plowing through it.

- **Pawn it.** "Pawning" originates from exercise physiology, where researchers have found (unsurprisingly) that people tend to stick with exercise regimens if they're financially penalized for slacking off. Give your friend some of your money—enough so that it will hurt if you never get it back (like grocery money for a month)—and say, "I'm going to finish a certain project by this deadline. At the end of that time, I will report to you. If I finish the project, return my money; otherwise, donate it to an organization that I despise." Money can be a strong motivator when your heart isn't.

Making an Action Plan

You've made it this far, so don't procrastinate this last important step. The procrastination profile that you started earlier should have three lists:

What do I put off?

How do I stall?

Why do I procrastinate?

Complete your profile by adding the reasons that you put off certain tasks. Most important, identify the accompanying breakthrough strategies that you're going to use to overcome each barrier.

Barriers

Breakthroughs

A personal plan is all that most people need to follow to shed their procrastination habit. Now, put *your* plan into action.

CHAPTER 7

Giving Presentations and Speaking in Public

The techniques in this chapter will help you become a more effective speaker and build confidence. Your confidence will grow as you gain more experience. Keep in mind that you don't have to be perfect when you present (perfection is, in fact, greatly overrated). A misstep or two in delivery isn't likely to break your reputation or career. It may even serve to humanize you with your audience. Go easy on yourself, learn and grow from your experience, and move on.

Identify Your Audience

Suppose that you went out on a first date last night, and today you're telling someone about it. How would you alter your story if that someone was your best friend? Your mother? A work colleague? A cute stranger? You'd change your word choices, your tone, and some of the details to fit your audience.

Thinking in terms of your audience is a crucial step in preparing your speech or presentation. Before you write a word, develop an audience persona. An audience persona is an individual representation of your entire audience. It changes the large, faceless group in front of you into the face of one person. Imagining one person:

- Makes writing and delivering your speech easier

- Helps you keep a consistent tone

- Helps you develop a more personal connection

To develop a persona, do research and ask questions to understand your audience as thoroughly as you can. For example, start by asking the event coordinator a general question like, "Tell me everything you can about the audience. Who are they?" After uncovering some broad commonalities, dig deeper by asking questions about the areas listed below. You should be able to flesh out some personal details to help you imagine a unique and interesting character (persona) to talk to. What are their political leanings? What TV shows do they watch? Do they listen to talk radio? Do they use Facebook to promote their businesses? These details may have nothing to do with the topic of your speech, but they can help you decide which stories and anecdotes to tell to help you connect emotionally with your audience.

Developing an Audience Persona

After asking general questions, ask about some of the following areas to discover nuances that can help you build a polished presentation.

Demographics

- Gender
- Age
- Marital status
- Number of children
- Nationality
- Ethnicity
- Geographic region
- Income level

Professional interests

- Industry or organization
- Level of seniority (student, intern, entry level, mid-level, senior)
- Field (administrative, clerical, office, technical, artistic, industrial, athletic, medical, legal, and so on)

- Advertising and marketing (TV, radio, print, billboards, press releases, social media, ad networks, and so on)

Personal information

- Media consumed (TV shows, movies, magazines, newspapers, radio, social media)
- Biggest influencers
- Business aspirations
- Biggest concerns
- Least concerns
- Common areas of concern

Everyday life

- Typical workday
- Dress (casual, business casual, business formal)
- Commute (personal car, public transit, telecommute)
- Eat and drink
- Work environment (office, retail, factory, outdoors)
- Types of homes and neighborhoods
- Recreation and entertainment preferences

Understand the Venue

What kind of room you will be presenting in? If possible or practical, take a two-minute walk through the presentation space prior to your talk. Whether or not you can inspect the venue in advance, prepare a room checklist before every presentation. A checklist (see below) makes it less likely that you'll forget batteries, backup devices, and other small things that can make a big difference. Many hotel and conference center websites provide room floor plans so that you'll know exactly what to expect. If possible, examine the online floor plan, then speak to somebody to confirm your findings.

Audience dynamics matter when you're creating a presentation. A large audience sitting theater style in a darkened room is going to be less conversational and interactive than a small audience sitting at tables in a well-lit room.

Use the checklist to ask about any equipment you might need. For most out-of-town business presentations, an event or meeting coordinator can tell you what's available to you and what you'll need to bring yourself.

Even if you're already familiar with the room, always bring a printed checklist, just to make sure you haven't forgotten any small details that can enhance the audience experience.

Venue Checklist

Room dynamics

- What is the size and shape of the room?

- How many seats?

- Is there a raised stage, or is the speaker on the same level with the audience?

- What is the floor plan?

- Does the room contain hindrances or obstructions? (view-blocking columns, a loud HVAC system, ambient light from windows, and so on)

Audience dynamics

- What is the audience setup? (theater style, classroom style, individual desk–chair sets, shared tables with chairs, desks with computer monitors, boardroom style, and so on)

- Will the audience be in the dark or in the light?

- Will the audience be eating or drinking?

- Will some audience members be remotely located? (speakerphone, video conference)

Equipment and technology

- Microphone type (wireless handheld, lavalier, podium, stand-up, wired, none)

- Computer type
- Presentation software on computer
- Computer projector type
- A/V cords
- Projection screen or monitor
- Blackboard
- Whiteboard
- Erasers
- Markers
- Clicker
- Extension cords
- Batteries
- Projector bulbs
- Laser pointer
- Overhead projector
- DVD player
- Television
- Speakerphone
- Lectern
- Podium
- Internet access
- Backup devices (flash drive, CD, DVD, and so on)
- Video cameras
- Audio recorders
- Other

Establish Personal Credibility

You have only a few seconds to convince your audience that you're worth listening to. Often, you can earn credibility before you even step up to the microphone by relying on an introduction. This technique is common in show business and in conferences, where an MC introduces a performer with a little hype or a moderator reads a speaker bio outlining experience, education, and other credentials.

If no third party is available to help establish your credibility, you can do it yourself (without simply reading your bio or bragging about your accomplishments). Use the following cues to build your credibility in a few seconds by demonstrating both confidence and competence.

To signal confidence:

- **Dress to inspire confidence.** Dress appropriately for the audience in front of you. If you're speaking to a large group of colleagues, business casual might be right. In another situation, like a formal press conference, you might have to wear a business suit. Before you agree to speak, find an insider who will tell you what kind of apparel is appropriate for your audience.

- **Look at your audience.** Stand up straight with your hands relaxed and at your sides. Make eye contact with an audience member. Let the audience look at your confident body language. Don't be in a rush to speak. Use a second or two of silence to grab the attention of your audience.

- **Sound confident.** The first words out of your mouth need to be bold, clear, and strong. Before you hit the stage, complete vocal warmups (page 67) and take a sip of room-temperature water.

To demonstrate competence:

- **Talk only about topics you understand.** Never agree to speak on a topic that you know little about or can claim no firsthand experience. If you're asked to speak about job-interviewing skills, but you haven't interviewed for a job for 15 years, decline the invitation or offer to talk about a related topic that you know about (body language, for example).

- **Tell the audience why you're competent.** Find one or two pertinent details in your background that relate to the subject matter. The audience doesn't need your complete resume, just a brief detail or two—if your education or job experience is irrelevant, don't mention them. For example, start a presentation on teaching border collies how to catch frisbees by saying, "I've been teaching border collies how to do tricks for 22 years. I'm Tom Garner, and let me tell you what I know about it."

Collect Ideas

Your brain is better at generating ideas than storing them. The best places to collect your ideas are often low-tech. Carry around a small notebook or pad of sticky notes for jotting down ideas, articles, and stories as they come to you.

High-tech approaches are also helpful. The moment you know that you'll be delivering an upcoming presentation, for example, create a cloud-based text file or document file with the title of your presentation. This file gives you a place to store any related ideas that you encounter. Cloud-based files can be accessed from any device that you happen to be using.

The goal here is to open your mind to receiving ideas as you go about your day, and then immediately note these ideas as they come to you. If you don't write down ideas, you'll almost certainly forget them by the time you sit down to write your presentation.

Three types of ideas are generally best to make note of:

- **Facts and information.** Bookmark articles, whitepapers, statistics, books, and blog posts that can enrich your presentation.

- **Stories.** Look, listen, or eavesdrop for stories people tell each other and things you see in the news. Or note your own recollections of past experiences.

- **Things that inspire.** Look for anything offbeat or unusual that inspires you. It may or may not belong in your presentation, but the fact that you noticed it is important. If it resonated emotionally with you, it may help you connect with your audience.

Think of idea-collection as brainstorming. You won't use every idea you jot down, and some of them will be silly, but when you sit down to assemble your presentation, you'll have a rich trove of material to work from.

Develop Your Story

The promise of a story rivets people's attention. To find a story buried in a mass of facts and statistics, look for a story trigger. In its simplest form, a story trigger is "something happened to someone." Even a dry fact like "sales increased by 14 percent" contains a story trigger: "sales increased by 14 percent" is the "something," and your firm is the "someone."

Whenever you see or hear a story trigger, ask questions to get to the underlying story:

- Why did sales jump?

- Why did it happen to your firm?

- Is the sales department doing something differently?

- Did a particular salesperson have an unusually good month?

- Did one of your competitors go out of business?

- Did you take advantage of a competitor's misfortune?

- Did something unexpected happen with the weather or the economy?

Find out why, what, who, when, where, and how. After that, it's a matter of sharing the story with your audience. Look for two types of story plots in particular:

- **Overcoming obstacles.** A child defeats a monster. A climber braves treacherous obstacles to reach a mountain peak. A salesperson defies a failing economy to increase sales by 28 percent.

- **Using creativity.** A detective solves a mystery. A hero saves the town. An accountant finds a novel way to shelter profits. Audiences love tales of ingenuity and creativity, not dry recitals of facts and numbers.

When designing your presentation, look for every opportunity to tell a story. When you have to share a fact with your audience, look in your idea file to find a story that supports that fact.

Create a Storyboard

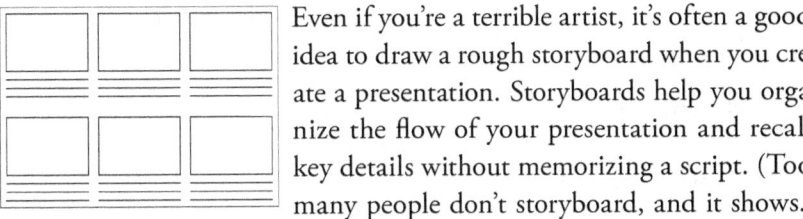

Even if you're a terrible artist, it's often a good idea to draw a rough storyboard when you create a presentation. Storyboards help you organize the flow of your presentation and recall key details without memorizing a script. (Too many people don't storyboard, and it shows.) A storyboard contains places for you to place pictures and their accompanying words.

In the picture area, draw or insert a representation of what the audience sees as you speak. Near the picture, write a short synopsis of what you'll be discussing or write your entire script. If you think visually or are a raconteur, you may be able to recall an entire story to tell about an image if you see only a photo, drawing, or chart. If this is the case, you can write, say, "Tell the story about X and how I reacted" on the storyboard instead of writing a detailed script to accompany the image.

Storyboards are also useful when you have little time to prepare a presentation. If you have only a few hours to develop a short speech, for example, grab some sticky notes out of your stock of ideas and arrange them in storyboard order. Use each sticky note to kick off a short anecdote to tell the audience—it's easier to tell a few small stories than to sit down and write a complete speech.

Storyboards can also be highly complex. If your audience is a group of technicians who need to know how to do highly detailed and specific steps, then your storyboard should show every step of the process, be carefully worded, and contain an image of what the technician would see during the process.

In general, start with a loose storyboard to provide a sense of flow and structure. As the presentation develops, fill in the details as needed.

Rehearse

Here are some rehearsal tips that can improve the emotional power of your final presentation:

- **Keep rehearsals real.** Keep your rehearsal as close to the real thing as you can. Find out whether you'll be sitting or standing and rehearse in that position.

- **Do a dress rehearsal.** Rehearse in the actual clothes you'll be wearing, including your shoes. Your performance will improve just by understanding how your body feels in full costume, even if your costume is a formal business suit instead of business casual. Small details matter here.

- **Use a real audience.** An audience in the room gives you emotional energy. If you don't have real people handy, hang pictures of friends, family, or colleagues, and pretend you're talking to them. Looking at faces you know and like gives your voice and body language more confidence and emotional power.

- **Record and watch yourself.** Record yourself on video during rehearsal. Watch to find areas where you can improve. This video is for your eyes only and doesn't need to be professionally shot. A video will help you see yourself as others do.

- **Listen to yourself.** Put the audio track of your recording on a portable device and then listen to it as you take a walk. If you find areas that drag, rewrite them. Listening to only audio helps you spot pace and pitch problems, and also helps you later recall the words and inflections that work well.

- **Rehearse in real time.** If you're giving a one-hour presentation, record a one-hour video of yourself. Start at the beginning and rehearse until the end. You can't chop up your presentation in front of a live audience, so don't chop up your rehearsals either. Also, rehearse at the same energy level that you're going to have for the presentation. If your presentation is at 10:00 AM, rehearse at 10:00 AM; if it's at 4:00 PM, rehearse at 4:00 PM.

Ready Your Voice

Warm up your voice before you present. Early-morning presentations are often the toughest. Don't subject your audience to throat-clearing or rough morning voice. Here are some tips for readying your voice for morning presentations:

- **Get moving early.** Get up and get moving. The steam from a hot shower can help you clear your voice.

- **Avoid cold drinks.** You want to warm your vocal chords, not cool them. Drink room-temperature water to clear any morning roughness in your throat.

- **Sing, talk, or hum.** Use your voice before you deliver your presentation. Sing or hum in the shower. Practice the opening lines of your presentations aloud in the car on the way to your presentation.

For late-day presentations, your voice may sound tired or ragged. Here are some tips for readying your voice for afternoon or evening presentations:

- **Save your voice.** Talk, sing, or hum a little throughout the day to keep your voice warm, but try not to talk too much during the day.

- **Avoid caffeine and carbonation.** Drink room-temperature water. Avoid coffee and cold cola, even if you're tired. If your voice is already strained later in the day, coffee can dry it out further, making it sound a little worse. Caffeine can compound any pre-presentation jitters, making your voice sound shaky. Also, avoid cold beverages, especially carbonated ones. Carbonation can cause you to micro-burp while you're talking.

Adjust the Microphone

"Can you all hear me OK?" is a weak opening statement that wastes your audience's time. Here are some tips for using a microphone:

- **Test it, use it.** If someone offers you a microphone, test it, and, if it works, use it. Take a few minutes to set up and test the mic before you present, not after you start. Let an audio technician or event coordinator help make you look and sound good. If the event coordinator asks you whether or not you want to use the mic, the correct answer is always yes. If someone (event coordinator or audience member) requests that you use the mic, don't argue.

- **Don't fear the mic.** The main reason that many presenters are microphone-shy is because they're secretly afraid of the mic. We're accustomed to hearing our own voices without amplification. With a mic, our voices sound loud and imposing to our own ears. If you're not familiar with the sound of your amplified voice, it can sound intimidating. But remember, it sounds loud to you, not to your audience. To lose your fear of the microphone, take a few moments before your presentation to get familiar with it. Run an audio check prior to the presentation. This check not only confirms that the equipment is working, but also makes you comfortable with using the mic.

- **Lavalier mics.** In large public-speaking venues, you may be asked to use a wireless lavalier mic (also called a lapel mic). A lavalier frees your hands and lets you use a broad range of body motions. If hooking up the mic involves dropping wires beneath your shirt, you can take the mic to a private place to attach it. The battery pack portion of the lavalier needs to hook on to a firm belt line, so pants or a sturdy skirt is needed (dresses and lavaliers don't mix). Because the wires in the pack are often behind your back, it can be hard to see where you might have gone wrong with a self-setup. Look in a mirror or ask a person you trust if your lavalier mic looks okay.

- **Handheld mics.** If someone gives you a handheld mic before a presentation, say a few sentences to get comfortable and to understand how close to hold the mic to your mouth. It's usually a lot closer than you think, which might affect your physical performance.

Manage Your Anxiety

Even the most experienced speakers, singers, actors, and entertainers get the jitters before their public performances. The first step to coping with anxiety is accepting that nervousness is a natural part of performing. Here are some tips for managing your anxiety:

- **Gain experience.** Experience is the number one way to rise above anxiety. As you gain experience, you gain confidence, and the more confidence you develop, the less likely you are to be thrown.

- **Improve your posture.** Some on-stage body postures can make you feel more afraid, whereas others can help you control your nerves. One of the worst and most common body postures for frightened speakers is head tipped down, hand clasped in front. This posture signals fear, not just to your audience but to your own body. Instead, do the opposite: place your hands behind your back and look up. This posture instantly makes your physical presence bigger and bolder, signals more confidence, and lets you take in more oxygen to better control your speaking.

- **Breathe.** If you're so nervous before a presentation that you feel nauseous, try blowing repeatedly on your thumb as if it's a birthday candle you're trying to blow out. This quick breathing exercise tends to calm your diaphragm while narrowing your focus.

Make a Strong Opening

The first words out of your mouth are hugely important. Always start your presentation with a cold open, in which you jump into the topic with no initial hemming, hawing, "Welcome," "Thank you," or any niceties or platitudes that lose your audience immediately. Here are five effective ways to start your presentation:

- **Ask an open-ended question.** Start your presentation with an open-ended question such as, "How can you use your writing skills to make extra money?" This question creates a mini mystery. It opens the knowledge gap and makes the audience wonder about how you'll close that gap. Note that open-ended questions can't be answered with a yes or no. For example, don't ask, "Can you use your writing skills to make extra money?" A close-ended question like this doesn't create a mystery, so the audience can mentally answer yes or no and quit paying attention.

- **Start with a story.** Start your presentation with a story or anecdote that illustrates a key point of your presentation. Starting with a story serves two purposes. First, people perk up whenever somebody begins to tell a story. Second, a well-told story often creates a sense of mystery; your audience will wonder how the content of your presentation will relate to your opening story.

- **Make a bold statement.** Start your presentation with a bold statement, such as, "The first words out of your mouth can make or break your presentation." A bold statement signals confidence, and it primes the audience to expect to hear how you'll be backing up such a strong assertion.

- **Imagine something.** Tell your audience to imagine something. Tell them to think of a situation, pretend to be somewhere, or imagine someone. For example, "Imagine you are in a giant auditorium. A thousand people are waiting to hear your first words." The moment somebody tells you to imagine something, it's almost impossible not to. Almost instantly, your audience is a part of your presentation. They're empathizing and engaging with the content of your speech because they're actually putting themselves in it.

- **Hard evidence.** Start with hard evidence, usually in the form of a quote or a documented fact. A hard-evidence opener is riskier than the preceding cold-opening techniques because the quote is often perceived as tired or hackneyed. Make sure that the quote's content, context, and author offer credibility to your presentation. Similarly, starting with a documented fact can also be risky. An obvious fact won't grab your audience's attention. Make sure it's a surprising or unexpected fact that defies common knowledge. Your fact must have enough of a shock value to ensure a powerful opening statement.

When you work on your next presentation, write five cold opens that use each of the preceding techniques. You can use only one cold open in your final presentation, of course, but going through this exercise may help you discover a stronger opening than you previously thought possible.

Tease Your Agenda

Most people won't even attend a meeting unless they know the agenda, and the best time to introduce an agenda is well before your presentation. Your agenda must state:

- The purpose of the presentation
- The topics to be discussed
- The names of the participants
- The duration of the presentation

For most business meetings and presentations, make sure that your audience has this agenda in writing before you present. In most cases, if your audience can see a written agenda before your presentation, you don't need to introduce the agenda. You can simply refer to it during your presentation to keep everyone on track. Starting your presentation by restating any portion of the agenda is redundant and risks losing your audience immediately.

During the presentation, use teasers to build interest in upcoming agenda items. A teaser gives the audience a bit of information that makes them want to know more, keeping them alert and interested. A good teaser might be, "We have some exciting news from our sales department, which I'll share with you after we discuss quarterly results."

Avoid Common Mistakes

The first words out of your mouth are the most important of your entire presentation. Your opening is where you have the best (and possibly only) chance to earn the attention and interest of your audience. In "Make a Strong Opening" on page 69, you learned how to use a cold opener to kick off your presentation. Now here's what *not* to say in the first few seconds:

- **Unoriginal phrases.** Never open with a few trite sentences—especially, "Hello! Thank you for the warm introduction. It's great to be here." How many times have you heard a speaker say something like this? An audience tends to mentally check out during those first few awkward sentences. To convince yourself, record the first minute or so of your speech. Start by saying a few polite words. Then try again by using a cold opener. After you see, hear, and feel the difference, you'll never go back to offering your audience an awkward or insincere nicety when you can grab them with power and confidence.

- **Clearing your throat.** No one wants to hear you clear your throat, especially not as the first noise out of your mouth. Throat-clearing is usually a sign of nervousness or is an uppity way to get attention. Warm up your voice before you take the stage (page 67).

- **Technical issues.** Don't draw attention to technical insecurities. "Is this thing on? Can you hear me in the back? Should I use the mic? Can you see my slides?" These opening comments indicate a strong disrespect for the audience by signaling that the speaker didn't bother to do audiovisual checks prior to the presentation. Don't waste your audience's time. Resolve all technical issues before your presentation.

- **Telling a joke.** Don't open your presentation with a joke, regardless of whether you have (or think you have) a great sense of humor. Having a sense of humor doesn't mean that you can tell a joke. Displaying some offbeat humor during your presentation can go over well, but starting with a joke almost always bombs. Big time. Groans, nervous laughter, and stony silence are a lot more common than genuine laughter. And in any case, it's hard to transition smoothly to a speech after a joke. Leave jokes to comedians.

Vary Your Vocal Patterns

A monotonous tone and a lack of dynamic range can make your audience fight to stay awake. A fundamental way to gain attention is to break your vocal patterns in the following ways:

- **Volume.** Vary the volume (dynamic range) of your voice. A sudden quiet, dramatic pause in your speech can capture just as much attention as if you suddenly spoke loudly. Find places in your presentation to insert a dramatic pause, raise your voice, or whisper an aside.

- **Tone.** Tone of voice is often driven by emotion. As an exercise, say, "I won the lottery" with various levels of feeling. Matter-of-factly: "I won the lottery." Excitedly: "I won the lottery!" Incredulously: "I won the lottery?" Say it with other emotions as well. You'll hear how much your feelings drive your tone of voice. In your speech, use a tone of voice to match your emotion to your words. Your facial expressions and body language also often reflect the emotions that you're projecting.

- **Pace.** At various times during your speech, speed up or slow down your delivery. Pick up the pace to inject urgency or excitement, or slow down for dramatic emphasis.

Eliminate Er, Um, and Ah

The persistent use of filler words and sounds (er, um, ah, like, so) can distract or annoy your audience. Practice the following three mindfulness exercises to reduce verbal tics in your speech:

- **Listen to yourself.** Practice awareness during your everyday conversations. Look for circumstances and patterns where you say filler words or sounds.

- **Listen to rehearsals.** Practice awareness as you rehearse (page 66). When you review the video of your rehearsal, note when you use filler words. What patterns arise? How does your use of fillers during your speech compare with your use of fillers in everyday conversations?

- **Give yourself a break.** A few ums and ers aren't going to ruin your presentation. It's likely that they won't even be noticed.

If the preceding mindfulness exercises didn't significantly reduce your verbal tics, dive a little deeper:

- **Try to relax.** If you notice that you tend to use more filler words when you're nervous or under pressure, relax—you're normal. Most people who undergo mindfulness exercises find that increased stress leads to more ums. Try reducing the stress with some positive reinforcement (for example, tell yourself, "OK, that's my last um for the day").

- **Reduce or avoid stress.** You can greatly minimize the stress of public speaking by properly rehearsing your presentation (page 66). Your use of filler words and sounds will drop dramatically.

- **Tell stories.** Don't use bullet points or lists when you can tell stories instead (page 64). Many speakers tend to emit an um prior to reading each bullet or list item, but can tell stories with little or no verbal fillers. Review your presentation and find any areas where you're reading bullet points or a list. Eliminating these items not only eliminates the ums from your presentation, but also helps you to better engage your audience by telling stories.

Communicate via Body Language

For the most part, you're better off not actively thinking about your body language. You don't want to become self-conscious. Instead, practice speaking from a place of confidence. When you connect emotionally with the words you're saying, your body naturally knows what to do. If you're having trouble building confidence, try these body-language tweaks:

- **Adopt a confident posture.** Stand up straight. Make eye contact with the audience. Find a few audience members who appear to like you, and look to them for support throughout your presentation. Their positive energy can help you feel more upbeat.

- **Don't fidget.** Avoid doing anything with your body that's distracting. Don't tug your hair, stuff your hands in your pockets, shuffle your feet, fumble with your keys, or toy with your jewelry. Fidgeting draws attention away from your message.

- **Record and watch your rehearsals.** You'll be the first one to notice anything distracting that you're doing with your body.

- **Write believable content.** Authentic body language tends to flow from content. When you feel confident about what you're saying, your body language will reflect that feeling and be more natural and believable. Don't try to adopt specific postures to accompany your words; it almost always looks forced and unnatural.

Use Visual Aids and Props

If you're going to use props in your presentation (such as a prototype product or an envelope on a nearby table), have a good reason to do so. In general, there are three reasons why you might want to use a prop:

- **Demonstration.** For most demos, showing is far more effective than telling. Audiences want to see and even interact with the prop that's being demoed.

- **Concrete metaphor.** If you want to talk about market share, for example, show your audience a chart. Props like diagrams, charts, and photos help the audience visualize abstract and numerical concepts.

- **Dramatic effect.** Use a prop when you want to provoke an emotional response. One TED speaker didn't just simply tell his audience that mosquitoes cause malaria, he opened a jar and told them that he had just released a few mosquitoes into the room.

If you do use a prop in your presentation, do the following:

- **Rehearse with your prop.** Practice, practice, practice. If you present yourself as an authority on how to use the prop, know exactly how it works and how to recover if things go wrong.

- **Present the prop effectively.** Apple CEO Steve Jobs told his audience that a new product was so thin that it could fit into an interoffice envelope. He held up the envelope and then slowly revealed the new product, a MacBook Air, to the crowd. Keeping your prop hidden and performing a dramatic reveal can build anticipation and add to the excitement of a new product or award announcement.

- **Treat every slide as a prop.** If your slide or prop doesn't demonstrate something, serve as a metaphor, or add dramatic effect, you probably should omit it from your presentation.

Deal With Technical Problems

Defective remote controls. Dead displays. Blown bulbs. Broken microphones. Technology and equipment fails, and how you deal with technical mishaps reveals your professionalism and confidence. Here's how to keep your cool:

- **Overprepare.** Use a checklist to make sure that you have everything you need to present, including backups. Show up early and test everything. Don't trust the assurances of event coordinators that software, hardware, and equipment will all work flawlessly.

- **Pack your own items.** If you can, bring some of your own items, such as your laptop and remote. Even if you don't need them for your presentation, having them on hand gives you a quick backup plan in case somebody else's equipment fails.

- **Know your presentation cold.** If the presentation technology fails during a live performance, go on without it. If the display goes dark, for example, continue the session while the tech staff works on the problem.

- **Involve the audience.** If the technology fails so completely that you can't salvage the presentation, get your audience involved in the problem. Business audiences are especially empathetic to technical problems (it's happened to all of them at some point). Involving your audience can also create a memorable emotional bond with them.

Take Questions

The question-and-answer (Q&A) portion of a presentation lets the audience members and the presenter hear different voices and perspectives. A well-done Q&A period is an interactive and lively part of the program. To keep your Q&A session energetic and enlightening, do the following:

- **Announce Q&A at the beginning.** If you're planning a Q&A, tell your audience near the very beginning of your presentation. For a small boardroom-style or classroom-style presentation, you might tell your audience to just jump in and ask questions at any time. For more-formal presentations, your audience is often better served when you tell them you'll answer their questions near the end. Announcing a Q&A usually ensures that the audience will think of good questions.

- **Hold Q&A *near* the end.** Hold your Q&A session near the end, not at the end. Don't close your presentation with Q&A; instead, tell your audience that you have one final thought to leave them with, but before you do, you'll open up the floor for questions. This near-the-end approach does two things. First, if no one has questions, you can proceed smoothly to your closing statement. Second, you control the final words—the last thing the audience hears is your message in your voice. Don't leave the last words to the whim of the last questioner.

As audience members start asking you questions, keep the following in mind as you answer:

- **Repeat or reframe.** Depending on the room and the size of the audience, you'll often want to repeat or reframe the question aloud. If you're speaking to a large audience and the questioner isn't using a microphone, repeating the question lets the rest of the audience hear. Also, if the question is awkwardly framed, instead of merely repeating the question, you can rephrase it in a way that the audience might better understand.

- **Answer briefly.** The best Q&A sessions are lively and interactive. You'll want to engage as many people as you can. Answer a question in a minute or less. If you don't think you can answer briefly, say so. A bit of humor can help. You can acknowledge that it's a complicated question and a comprehensive answer might take an hour. Instead, tell your audience you'll give them the short answer and that in the interest of time, you'll take another question.

- **Take control.** Every so often an audience member will ask you a long, incoherent, rambling, or off-topic question. The rest of the audience wants this person to stop talking just as much as you do. If a person can't ask a question in under thirty seconds, politely but firmly shut them down. Tell them that you're going to interrupt them. Don't *ask* if you can interrupt them—tell them. Remind them that time is limited and that out of respect for the audience, you're going to need to move on to another question or close the presentation. This may sound harsh or rude, but your audience will love you for doing it. If you truly feel that this approach is too harsh, you can try softening it by adding that you will be available to take their question after the presentation; however, do so only if you actually have the time and inclination to meet with the person afterward.

Close Strongly

You have dozens of ways to end your talk with a bang. Here are a few simple closing ideas to consider:

- **Short summary.** The easiest way to close is with a short summary. If your presentation features three key takeaways, for example, close by reminding your audience what those three points were.

- **Restate the title.** If your speech has a provocative or entertaining title, close by dramatically restating or reframing the title. For example, in a presentation titled *Writing a Screenplay in Six Weeks*, you might close with, "Thank you! Now go out and write a screenplay."

- **Call to action.** Closing with a call to action is particularly effective if you want the audience to do something as a result of your presentation. Close by telling your audience exactly what to do, as well as how and when to do it.

- **A personal tagline.** Ending with a personal tagline is effective if you often present to the same audience. A sales manager can end every sales meeting by saying, "Sell value" (or whatever). The drumbeat of a few distinctive words can make you and your message more memorable. It also lets the group know that you've wrapped up your presentation.

- **A quote.** Closing with a quote can be a satisfying option for the audience. Unlike an opening quote (page 69), an effective closing quote doesn't offer any surprising new insights. Rather, it summarizes the main thrust of your presentation. Be sure that the content, context, and author offer credibility, as well as closure, to your presentation.

- **A final story.** A final story needs to be emotionally powerful or provide closure on a story you may have opened up earlier in your speech.

In addition to speaking your final words aloud, you have the option of displaying them on their own closing slide.

When you work on your presentation, write at least three different closings that use any of the preceding techniques. You can use only one closing in your final presentation, of course, but going through this exercise may help you discover a stronger closing than you previously thought possible.

To wrap up your presentation, say your closing words, look at your audience, pause for a moment of silence, and then nod, bow, or use other body language to let your audience know that your speech is over.

Get Feedback

Feedback (positive or negative) can be a gift that helps you become a better speaker. A helpful review is:

- **Truthful.** If written feedback states, "Don't stand in front of your slides; it's distracting," and you really did stand in front of your slides, then that's valuable feedback—you're not going to do that again. On the other hand, if the feedback states, "The misspelled words on your slides made you look unprofessional," and your slides had no misspellings, then there's nothing you can do but ignore the reviewer. Don't sweat an untruthful review for a moment.

- **Specific.** General rants and raves don't offer specific advice on how to improve your next performance. If someone punctuates their written feedback with exclamation points and uses abstract terms like "love" and "brilliant," then you're not getting specific advice about how to improve your performance. Don't take ego-stroking feedback too seriously. And certainly don't take trollish "hate"- and "stupid"-laden rants at all seriously or let them hurt your confidence. No matter how well you did, you're not going to please everyone. It may be that you're delivering a hard truth, or maybe the reviewer is offended or just plain mean. If you receive a few negative evaluations that differ considerably from the bulk of your reviews, it's not *you* that has a problem. However, honest critiques that point out areas where you can improve are good news—use this feedback to improve your next performance.

CHAPTER 8

Speed Reading and Strong Recall

If you love reading or you're hungry for knowledge, then speed reading is a skill you can benefit from. This chapter teaches you simple, proven techniques to improve how fast you absorb information, while boosting your comprehension and retention. You'll also find plenty of practice drills and exercises to reinforce your new skills.

Practice What You Learn

To improve in any worthwhile skill, you must practice what you learn. As you make your way through this chapter, you'll encounter a variety of techniques and exercises to help you become a more efficient reader. In most cases, you'll be asked to practice by using your own reading material. Use material that you normally read, whether it's for school, work, or personal reading.

The exercises will improve your reading in three areas:

- Speed

- Comprehension

- Retention

With time and practice, you'll find yourself reading significantly faster, while also improving your comprehension and retention of the material.

Measure Your Reading Speed

To measure your current reading speed, choose some unchallenging, non-technical material and read it for exactly one minute (set a timer). Read at a comfortable speed, neither faster nor slower than you normally would. And read for good comprehension. When one minute is over, mark the spot where you stopped reading, and then go back and count the words. If you read something on your computer or the web, you can copy and paste the words into a word processor or *wordcounter.net* for an automated word count.

The average person reads somewhere in the range of 150–250 words per minute. Regardless of whether you're at, above, or below average, this chapter will help you improve. You now know your starting point, and can measure your progress.

Habits That Slow You Down

Three common reading habits may be slowing you down:

- **Fixating.** Your eyes fixate on each word as you read. When you first learn how to read a language, fixation is necessary to break each word down to its syllables. But as you become fluent in the language, you don't have to fixate because you can read groups of words. You already read groups of words routinely. Suppose that you're driving a car and you see a sign that says "West Palm Beach." Your eyes are initially fixated on the road ahead, but as the sign comes into view, your eyes will fixate only once on the sign, and you'll read those three words easily in one fixation. If those same words were in the middle of a paragraph, however, you might fixate on every word. That's a leftover reading habit that you must break if you want to read faster. Later lessons will help you read groups of words (page 85).

- **Regressing.** You go back to reread material. We've all read an entire page of text and then stopped to think, "What did I just read?" The issue is concentration. Your mind wanders while reading, especially if the material is dry or uninteresting. Later lessons will help you improve your focus.

- **Subvocalizing.** You say every word in your head as you read. This habit is common among almost all readers, and it's the one that most slows us down. You've seen most of the words that you read hundreds or thousands of times, so you don't have to say a word in your head to understand it. When you're driving a car and see a stop sign, for example, you don't say "stop" in your head. But if the word "stop" appears in the middle of a paragraph, and you say it in your head, then you're subvocalizing. If you say every word in your head, you can read only as fast as you talk. The average reading speed is 150–250 words a minute. And average talking speed is 150–250 words a minute. Exactly the same. Why? Because most readers subvocalize, which limits their reading speed. You can read faster than you can talk because you can think faster than you can talk. Later lessons will help you still your inner voice.

Using Your Hand to Guide Your Eyes

The simplest thing that you can do to improve your reading speed is to use your finger or a pen to guide your eyes through the text. This technique improves your concentration while reading, which consequently improves your reading speed and comprehension.

Place your fingertip or pen point slightly below the text on a page and "underline" the words from left to right in one continuous motion. Don't actually look at your finger, but instead let it guide you from left to right, through the line of text. Your eyes, being naturally attracted to motion, will follow your finger through the material. Initially, you might feel slightly uncomfortable if you don't already read with your hand. But the more you do it, the more natural it becomes. Unsurprisingly, this technique works better on printed material than screen-based text.

Exercise: Read with your finger or pen for 15 minutes. You should find yourself better focused while reading. Some people notice an immediate improvement of 20 to 30 percent in their reading speed just by using their hand while reading.

Reading Faster on Screens

Multiple studies show that the average person reads about 20 to 30 percent slower on a screen as opposed to reading on the printed page. Here are a few tips for reading onscreen text:

- **Adjust the screen brightness.** When you read on a screen, a light is being beamed directly at your eyes, which can cause discomfort after reading for long durations. To reduce discomfort, adjust the screen brightness to the lowest comfortable level for the ambient light.

- **Reduce distractions.** Distractions are a major reason why people read more slowly on a screen. Distractions include ads, animations, and personal distractions (email, Facebook, pop-up notifications, and so on). The easiest way to get rid of webpage junk is to use a page-decluttering feature in your browser. In Apple's Safari browser, for example, use the built-in Reader feature. In Mozilla Firefox or Google Chrome, try Readability (*readability.com*). Personal distractions are a matter of self-discipline—close the offending browser tabs and applications, and turn on all your devices' do-not-disturb features.

- **Guide your eyes.** For gadgets with touchscreens, like the Apple iPad or Amazon Kindle, using your hand as a reading guide is impractical, so instead use the opposite end of a pen or stylus to guide your eyes. Move the pen lightly and smoothly across the screen so you don't scratch the surface. If you don't have a pen or it's impractical to use one, then instead use the fixation-points technique for reading groups of words (page 85). Most of the other techniques described in this chapter can be applied to reading on screens as well.

Drills That Boost Reading Speed

This lesson covers a basic drill that will help boost your reading speed. You can read on paper or on a screen. Use material that you normally read, whether it's for school, work, or personal reading. Make sure that you have enough material for 20 minutes of reading. The goal of this drill is to purposely read faster than you do normally and to become accustomed to seeing words at a faster rate.

Drill: Set a timer and read for 20 minutes with the goal of strong comprehension. Read at whatever speed feels comfortable, without going too fast or too slow. After 20 minutes, mark the place where you stopped and take a short break. Now, reread the same material in 10 minutes or less. Don't worry if your comprehension degrades—you're essentially skimming the material at about double your normal reading speed.

If you practice this drill, then eventually your normal speed will feel a bit slow. If you read normally at 200 words per minute, for example, this drill forces you to raise your speed to 400 words per minute or more. With practice, 200 words per minute will start to feel slow, and you'll be able to boost your new normal speed to, say, 250 words a minute without sacrificing comprehension. After you start reading comfortably with comprehension at 250 words a minute, practice speed drills at 500 words a minute and, eventually, 300 won't feel too fast.

This drill has another benefit: by skimming through material that you read already, you're essentially reviewing that material, which helps you recall it better in addition to improving your reading speed. To get the best results, practice this drill repetitively over time—ideally, every day for two weeks. To practice:

1. Read for 20 minutes

2. Speed through the material you just read in 10 minutes

3. Repeat steps 1 and 2

At this point, you will have done about 40 minutes of normal reading and 20 minutes of drill reading (one hour total). Repeating these steps results in gradual and consistent increases in your reading speed. Measure your reading speed daily to track your progress (page 82).

Reading Groups of Words

A common reason why people read slowly is because they read on a word-by-word basis. You can speed up your reading by learning how to read more than one word at a time. You already *do* read groups of words in a glance in some situations (such as reading road signs when you're driving), so you want to replicate this existing ability for normal reading. Here's a technique for reading groups of words:

1. Mentally break each line of text into three parts: a beginning, a middle, and an end. Each part is a fixation point.

2. Focus your eyes so that they make three fixations per line, once at the beginning, once in the middle, and once at the end.

3. During each fixation point, attempt to read the group of words in that area. Your goal is to read between three to five words per fixation.

If the lines are narrow (5–8 words per line), make only two fixations per line, on the first half and the second half of the line.

This technique may be challenging initially, but with practice you'll be able to read groups of words more easily.

Exercise: Read word groups for ten minutes (on paper or on a screen).

Using Deadlines to Improve Reading Speed

One way that you can read faster is to improve your focus by setting deadlines for yourself while reading.

Exercise: Time how long it takes you to read one page of text. Write down this number—it's your benchmark time. Going forward, you want to meet or beat this time reading different pages of similar length. Do this exercise repeatedly, timing how long it takes you to read each page. Little by little, successive reading times should lessen. To measure your progress, record all your times on a sheet of paper or on a spreadsheet.

Suppose that your benchmark time is one minute and seven seconds. An example tally might look like this after eight attempts:

Attempt	Time
1	1:07
2	1:04
3	1:10
4	1:03
5	1:01
6	1:01
7	0:59
8	0:55

Don't worry if any attempt takes you a little longer than an earlier one. As you continue practicing, and focusing intensely on a timed deadline, you'll find it easier and easier to get through the pages faster.

Start by tracking your times for only a single page of text because it provides immediate feedback. After a little practice, track your times while reading two or more pages. If a sentence continues from one page to the next, continue reading until you finish that sentence.

Practice this exercise for 15 minutes a day for two weeks. During this time, you'll find a gradual increase in your speed as you challenge yourself to get through the material in less time.

Previews and Overviews

The point of most reading is to learn or experience something new. Because most people are unfamiliar with their reading material, they tend to read linearly from beginning to end, slowly. If you don't know what to expect, you're going to read slower. Retention, a function of repetition, is also a problem. If you don't preview and overview the material, then you've had only one repetition and you'll likely forget much of what you read.

Previewing the Material

Previewing is a quick way to become somewhat familiar with information prior to an overview and a full read-through.

Suppose that you're about to read a simple one-page article. Preview it by reading the first sentence of every paragraph. Because first sentences tend to carry the main ideas, reading them initially supplies all or most of the main points.

To preview a chapter in a nonfiction book, read the introduction and conclusion. In a textbook, for example, the introduction might be titled Introduction or Objectives, and the conclusion might be titled Conclusion or Summary. If the chapter lacks clearly described titles for these sections, read something from the beginning and the end, such as the chapter's first few and last few paragraphs.

When you know what to expect from the material, you'll be able to read it a little faster than usual and with better comprehension. Retention is also improved, because repetition is part of this process.

Getting an Overview of the Material

After previewing the material, dig deeper to get an overview: read all the headings, subheadings, and bolded words. If your material isn't structured in this way, read the first sentence of every paragraph. If you come across charts, diagrams, or other figures, read only their titles or captions (don't analyze their content).

The goal of an overview is to find the most important concepts in the material. Getting an overview typically takes from one to five minutes, depending on the length and complexity of the chapter.

After you preview and overview the material, read it in its entirety. Your reading speed, comprehension, and retention will be considerably greater than if you had just read the material once with no preparation.

Comprehension vs. Retention

Comprehension and retention are different concepts and separate skills. Comprehension is what you understand *as* you read material. Retention is what you recall later. Passing a test on material that you read earlier, for example, is a matter of retention, not comprehension. Sometimes we can have excellent comprehension but poor retention. You can improve both of these skills.

Varying Reading Speed to Improve Comprehension

The easiest way to improve your comprehension with little to no practice is to vary your reading speed, slowing down at some points and speeding up at others. For example:

- Slow down on the first sentence of a paragraph and then speed up a little bit through the rest of the paragraph. For each new paragraph, repeat the process. The first sentence of a paragraph tends to be the main idea, or topic sentence, of that paragraph.

- If you're reading a novel, slow down a bit at the beginning of the story, speed up through the middle, and then slow back down near the end.

- If you're a student reading something that's likely to be on an exam, slow down a little bit through that section, and speed up through material that you're already familiar with.

Taking Notes to Improve Retention

Practice taking quick notes to help you recall reading material.

Exercise: Read a paragraph and then immediately jot down a brief note of what you just read. Then repeat the process: read the next paragraph, take a note, and so on. Write quick notes—just a word or a phrase that describes some of the content in that paragraph.

This exercise makes you pay attention to the material by constantly forcing you to ask yourself, "What did I just read?" With practice, you'll improve your ability to retain the information. Practice this exercise 15 minutes a day for two weeks. (This exercise is intended only for building skills, not for everyday reading.)

Part of the reason why we forget information is because usually we aren't paying attention. When you forget someone's name almost immediately after they tell it to you, that's probably for lack of attention. The same thing happens with reading. Note-taking helps you pay attention because if you know that you'll need to write something down, then you'll more likely pay attention while you're reading.

Memory and Retention

Several physiological systems work together to form memories by helping you create, store, and retrieve various pieces of information and experiences. These systems let us sort through an overwhelming amount of incoming information to find the most important things that need to be turned into memories. The three main types of memory are:

- **Sensory memory.** Sensory memory is the shortest-term element of memory (even shorter than short-term memory). It's the ability to retain impressions of sensory information that come from your five senses. Sight, hearing, smell, taste, and touch all create sensory memories that are held for no more than a few seconds. Your attention determines whether sensory information will be retained in your short-term memory, and you can use your senses to improve your attentiveness. To remember information or an experience, try to focus on all the sensory aspects of the situation. If you're reading something, for example, pay close attention to the visual structure of the page and the chapter. Focus on the smell and sounds of the surrounding environment. Then try to link those senses to the information you're reading.

- **Short-term memory.** Short-term memory is the capacity for holding a small amount of information in mind, in an active, readily available state, for a short period of time. It's where you hold information that needs to be used at the moment. You use your short-term memory for many functions, including reading, writing, planning, and mental math. Short-term memories expire in seconds. Unless you rehearse this information or commit it to memory in some other way, you'll forget it almost immediately.

- **Long-term memory.** Long-term memory is information stored in the brain that's retrievable over a long period of time.

Repetition is the single most important factor that determines whether memories change from short-term to long-term. If you're reading, you must have repetition involved to recall the information. Fortunately, it's unnecessary to read the material entirely five or ten times just to remember it. Instead, do a preview and an overview (page 87) to get three separate exposures to the material (preview + overview + full read). In many cases, these three repetitions will help you remember the information.

If you need to remember the information very well, take notes during this process to increase the number of repetitions. After you preview the material, take some general notes, and after you overview the material, take additional, more-detailed notes. That's four repetitions before you even read the material fully (preview + notes + overview + notes).

The final step is reading the information in its entirety. You can take still more notes at the end of sections or as you encounter notable information, which would further increase the number of repetitions. Make sure that your notes are quick and concise so they don't take too much time away from your reading.

This entire process provides you with at least six repetitions or exposures to the material (preview + notes + overview + notes + full read + notes). Contrast this method with the way most people read: from beginning to end, slowly, once, with little recall the next day.

More Retention Tricks

Here are a few more tricks to help you better retain what you read:

- **Talk.** Talk to another person about what you just read. When you put something into your own words and teach it to someone else, you're better able to remember that information.

- **Visualize.** Picturing something makes it easier to remember. It's easier to remember faces than names, for example. At the end of the paragraphs or sections you're reading, try to imagine the information visually.

- **Exaggerate.** We remember things that are out of the ordinary. Exaggerate whatever visualizations you make while reading. Picture something as very big, very small, or oddly colored, for example.

- **Associate.** Associate one thing you read to another thing you already know.

- **Chunk.** Chunking works well for recalling large amounts of complex information. If you're reading a 50-page chapter, for example, break it down into, say, five 10-page sections, and then apply the preview/overview/read-through process to those five chunked sections separately.

Memorizing Word Meanings

Technical terms, jargon, and words you've never seen before are bound to pop up in your reading material. If you can't figure out a word's meaning by its context (by reading the entire paragraph), then you'll have to look it up in a dictionary or reference.

Entire study guides are devoted to committing word meanings to memory. Search the web for *memorizing vocabulary words*, and you'll find lots of tricks and techniques that are superior to (and more entertaining than) rote memorization. My favorite technique involves word substitution, visualization, and association, in which you remember a word's definition by using similar sounds and whimsical mental images.

The word transient, for example, means "lasting only for a short time; impermanent." To remember the definition of this word, break it down into smaller substitute words by using the word's phonetic sounds, and then associate these words with the meaning of transient. For example, break down "transient" into "train" + "sees" + "ant," then conjure a mental image of a train bearing down on an ant crossing its path. The train engine, having eyes, sees the ant but can't stop, meaning the ant is a short-lived (transient) obstacle. Picture this image vividly in your mind's eye. Now, when you hear the word transient (train-sees-ant), you'll recall your image of the short-lived (transient) ant about to meet its doom.

The 80/20 Rule

Economists call it the Pareto principle, statisticians call it the power law, but most people call it the 80/20 rule (or, with gravitas, the law of the vital few). For our purposes, it means spending most of your reading time on the most important 20% of the material. During the preview and overview steps (page 87), focus on roughly 20% of the chapter in the hopes of getting 80% of the information. In some situations, you won't have to read the text in its entirety. If your goal is just to get the essence of the information, then you may only need to read about 20% of the material.

Reading a Book in a Day

You can get through a book or magazine in a day by using the preview technique (page 87) and the 80/20 rule (page 92). The following reading method is suitable for informational material, so apply it to non-fiction rather than fiction:

1. Read the back cover, the inside flap, and the table of contents to get an idea of what the book is about.

2. Read the introduction and conclusion of every chapter. If the chapters lack clearly specified introductions and conclusions, read the first three and the last three paragraphs of each chapter. By doing this, you're previewing the whole book and using the 80/20 rule.

Your goal is to get as much information about the book in as little time as possible. For many nonfiction books, this process takes 10–20 minutes. Even if it takes longer, you're still spending a relatively short amount of time consuming a lot of information.

You can use this strategy as a filter to determine which books are worth your time. Reading the introduction and conclusion of each chapter gives you much more than just the essence of the material. In many situations, you'll feel like you read nearly the whole book. If you do decide to read the entire book, you'll have a good idea of what it's about, letting you read it fast and with strong comprehension.

If you want to push yourself, try to read a book each day for seven days. If you're hungry for knowledge and love consuming information, you'll be surprised at how much you can consume in such little time.

Reading Different Types of Material

News. Most news articles are written with a structure known as an upside-down triangle—the most important information appears at the top of the article, followed by content of increasingly lesser importance. The who, what, where, when, and how all appear in the first few paragraphs.

To read a newspaper or news website quickly, apply the 80/20 rule (page 92) to get a general idea of what's happening in the news: read only the first two to three paragraphs of an article to get most of the information in the least time. Note that op-ed (opinion) pieces are structured with introductions and conclusions, not as upside-down triangles. News articles usually have short paragraphs (three or fewer sentences). Longer paragraphs typically indicate a thoughtful or substantive piece with an introduction and conclusion.

Magazines. Preview and overview (page 87) each article of interest in the magazine. For the preview, read the article's introduction and conclusion. If the article is short (say, ten or fewer paragraphs), then read only the first and last paragraphs. For the overview, read all the headings and the first sentence of every paragraph. Now you can decide whether the entire article is worth your time. To read multiple articles or the entire magazine, preview and overview all the articles first. From there decide which articles are worth reading entirely. To be even more efficient, set a 15-minute deadline (page 86) to preview and overview the entire magazine or every article of interest.

Textbooks and technical material. Preview and overview (page 87) each chapter to become familiar with information prior to a full read-through. Take notes to increase the number of repetitions (page 90) to boost retention. If the material includes figures, see "Charts, Diagrams, and Formulas" next.

Charts, Diagrams, and Formulas

You're reading through material and encounter the text, "Refer to Figure 3.5." Should you look at the figure when you're referred to it, or wait until the end of the sentence, paragraph, or page? The most effective strategy is to stop reading and refer to Figure 3.5 the moment that you read the words, "Refer to Figure 3.5." That's not what most people do, however—they read, "Refer to Figure 3.5" and keep reading without a glance at the figure.

When the text refers you to a figure, look at it briefly to get a first impression. If the next sentence says something like, "Figure 3.5 shows the relationship between X and Y," then stop reading again and check the figure to visually confirm this statement. If the sentence after that says, "Figure 3.5 also shows Z," then stop reading yet again and check the figure to confirm this new information.

Going back and forth between reading and checking figures might seem like a choppy way of reading, but it's an important way to boost your comprehension of charts, diagrams, and formulas. A picture is worth a thousand words. Any time that you can confirm information visually will help your comprehension immensely. You can stop referring to the figure after the text stops referring to it.

CHAPTER 9

Managing Up and Influencing Your Boss

People in workplace hierarchies often spend all or most of their time and attention focused downward on the people who report to them directly (their team). But that practice is usually self-limiting and opens the door to stress and surprises from above. A smarter strategy is to direct a healthy minority of your time upward by managing your boss proactively. Managing up, as it's often called, builds a productive relationship that helps both you and your boss. This chapter shows you how to manage your boss by using practical, proven techniques.

Understanding Yourself and Your Boss

Being an excellent leader means managing your boss (managing up) as well as your team (managing down). Managing up is a form of influence in which you act intentionally to help and persuade your boss in a manner that benefits you, your team, and your boss.

Managing up is a normal part of a professional relationship, and your boss—and boss's boss—are likely already skilled at influencing their superiors. To be clear, managing up doesn't explicitly involve looking for preferential treatment or taking credit for others' achievements. Your desired result is the best relationship that you can build. If you apply the techniques covered in this chapter consistently, you'll learn how to stay at the front of your boss's mind and keep informed about the information, gossip, and changes happening above you in the organization.

In time, you'll become more useful to your boss, very likely leading to increased opportunities for you. Managing up doesn't involve the loss of dignity through excessive brownnosing. Instead, it's about figuring out how to understand and be helpful to your boss.

Managing up differs considerably from managing your team:

- Usually, there's only one boss to manage as opposed to multiple team members.

- Your boss has more power and status than you do, which is the opposite of the situation with your team.

- Your boss has more personnel and budget responsibilities than you do.

- You don't understand your boss's world as well as you understand your team's world.

These differences mean that interacting with your boss entails more risk than managing your team, so deliberate when you devise your own strategy for managing up.

You may be thinking, "Why take the risk? I'll just keep my head down and run my team." But consider that the results produced by you and your team are local and can be underappreciated (or ignored) throughout the larger organization. That's where your boss comes in. When managed correctly, your boss becomes a strong catalyst—someone who can provide you with direct assistance, acquire needed resources, and advocate for you throughout the larger system.

Without too much effort, you can:

- Know your boss's motivations

- Understand your boss's challenges

- Gain clarity about your boss's expectations

- Know when and how to communicate with your boss

When it comes to your hiring plans, changes to your work processes, or nearly any workplace goal, no one is more important than your boss. Why do people quit jobs? Bad boss relationships. Why do people stay with jobs and forego other opportunities? Great boss relationships. So your wisest course is to manage up. The benefits far outweigh the small risks, and it's not that hard, as this chapter will make that clear. In time, managing your boss won't feel like a contrived attempt to persuade. It will feel like a normal part of a beneficial, two-way professional relationship.

To Know Others, First Know Yourself

Tailoring a productive and mutually beneficial relationship with your boss starts with understanding yourself, and deep self-knowledge comes from honest self-reflection. This section gets you started, but be prepared to devote a few minutes each day (about 30 to 60 minutes each week) sitting in a quiet place contemplating your inner and outer life.

Grab a pen and paper and contemplate where you are personally and professionally. How you feel about it? What should you do about it? This type of personal analysis is not only therapeutic, but it also helps you structure your thoughts and plans. Next, become more aware of the evidence and happenings that surround you. There's typically a lot of data to consider, for example:

- Your interactions with others at work

- Your performance evaluations

- 360-degree evaluation results

- Personality or aptitude tests that you've completed

- Awards that you have (or haven't) received

- Promotions that you have (or haven't) received

- Feedback sought from peers or your mentor

People view you differently than you think they do, and your goal is to get close to perceiving yourself as others do by evaluating yourself and the data honestly (if not always comfortably).

When you're at ease seeing yourself as others see you (for better or worse), then you're ready to start managing up. You'll know how to present yourself in the best way, given how your boss is likely to view you, and you'll be prepared to address nearly any major issue concerning you. You should also be able to articulate your short-term and long-term goals, for example, and explain how you learned from your biggest public mistakes.

Before you run off and start managing your boss, think about your professional network. Who in your network comes to mind as someone who your boss might want to know, or someone who might want to help your boss? Make a mental list of their names and skills, and be ready to use them. Don't randomly suggest that your boss might want to connect with so and so. Wait until there's a legitimate reason to suggest the connection in response to a problem or opportunity, then speak up.

Managing up isn't necessarily difficult. But however difficult it is, in many ways it's easier than honest self-reflection, so start now getting to know yourself better.

Assessing Your Social Capital

Before you interact with your boss, assess your social capital, which measures your:

- Latitude to say and do what you want at work

- Freedom to make decisions regardless of what others think

- Immunity to real repercussions from your decisions and recommendations

Your social capital is your single biggest intangible career asset. Think of it as chips in a poker game. Your stack is only so big and it's up to you to decide how much to bet and when. Social capital is easy to spend but it can be hard to recoup. Thus, think twice and act once to ensure that you're making wise decisions about when and how to manage your boss.

You have three main ways to build your social capital:

- **Do great work.** If you want more latitude to speak and act as honestly as possible, nothing works faster than creating a great performance track record.

- **Gain attention.** Increased social capital results from attention gained through awards and other public accomplishments, including winning awards at work, publishing a paper at a conference, and earning praise from a key customer. Don't spend excessive time chasing public accolades, however—doing exemplary work is the surer and faster path to attention.

- **Help others.** No matter how busy you are, find time to back up your peers. Be there when your boss needs someone to stay late or work the occasional weekend. When people see you behave consistently and helpfully, they'll be more willing to give you latitude when you spend a few chips.

You can estimate your current level of social capital by answering a few questions:

- Have you spent significant capital recently? If only a week ago you engaged your boss in a tough conversation about the need for change, then you should probably wait until you rebuild your pile of chips.

- Have the major indicators of your performance been rising, falling, or steady? Consider your evaluations, awards, promotions, and comments from your boss.

- How have people been interacting with you in the last few months? Are they eager to help you? Are they choosing you to help them? Are they connecting you to others in their professional network?

The answers should provide you with some confidence about whether your pile of chips is small, medium, or large.

Consider an example. The team has just vetted a group of candidates for a new hire and now the boss is about to make a decision. The boss favors the candidate who went to the same school that he did. The team wants someone else but they'll silently accept the boss's choice. What do you do? If you speak up, it will cost you some social capital and you don't know how your boss will react. If you think that speaking up might greatly reduce or wipe out your social capital, then acquiesce unless the issue is of great importance. On the other hand, if you feel that your pile of chips is large and your boss will be open to your feedback, then your risk is low.

We all have limited latitude to do and say what we'd like. Think carefully about how much social capital you have and whether or not the issue at hand is worth the chips. Your goal is to save your chips for the best bets that are most likely to pay off.

Learning Your Boss's World

To manage upward effectively, you must learn about your boss's reality. That world, with its different players, concerns, and dynamics, may vary considerably from yours. When you spend time learning this landscape, benefits accrue:

- Your boss will sense your thoughtful respect and understanding of his or her reality.

- Your insight into your boss's world signals your aspirations to play at that level.

- Your boss will feel a bit more understood and thus inclined to listen to what you have to say.

Understanding starts with executive-level communication. The way that you speak to your boss sometimes must differ from how you speak to your team. Keep three things in mind:

- **Be brief.** The higher up you go in the chain of command, the more precious time is as a resource, so respect that.

- **Be bottom-line oriented.** Don't delve into unnecessary details unless asked.

- **Talk the talk.** Very often, the vernacular changes across levels of the organization (in general, it becomes more formal at higher levels).

The players in your boss's world are different. The people are likely a little older, more experienced, often more educated, and their focus is on large internal systems and outside considerations, not inside groups and departments. The decisions have greater consequences than you're used to. Correct decisions mean increased revenue, higher profits, and job growth. Bad choices mean strained budgets and lost jobs. When you start managing upward, put your needs in perspective by considering what your boss has to deal with every day.

After surveying the big picture, dive down and examine your boss's smaller patterns, including:

- Calendar of activities

- Electronic flow of work

- Who is approached for projects

- Tasks given priority

- Favorite go-to people, tools, and methods

- Office arrival and departure times

- Lunch and break times and durations

When you plan when to talk to your boss about various issues, these little patterns are as important as anything else you'll consider.

Also, be sure to understand your boss's general calendar. Every organization has its own way of scheduling activities—the budget cycle, hiring patterns, audit processes, the employee evaluation system, and so on. Knowing when they occur and overlap gives you insight into your boss's overall workload at any given time.

Managing up means being consistently aware of how best to interact with your boss—knowing not only which issue to address, but when and in what context. When you're mindful of your boss's world as well as your own needs, it's amazing how much more they're willing to listen to what you have to say.

Understanding Your Boss's Motivations

Being an effective professional requires people skills, which you can hone by using logic and observation. The most common motivations that drive behavior are:

- **Need for attention.** Some people like to be noticed. They want praise. They want to look good in the eyes of others. They love winning and receiving awards. When you give them information or recommendations, ask yourself whether there are implications for the attention that they might receive.

- **Need for achievement.** People with a strong need for achievement want to master things and understand how things work. They want to earn credentials and certifications. And they love promotions. Think about whether your interactions with them feed that desire.

- **Desire for power and control.** Many people are driven by a disposition to be in charge. They like leading, structuring, and facilitating the work of others. They have strong confidence and are willing to accept the risks associated with making decisions for others. Think about how your interactions help or hurt their overall control at work.

- **Love of helping others.** For many people at different levels of the organization, a primary driver is the desire to reach out and assist others. They feel compelled to ensure the success of others as much as their own success. As everyone else considers the cost and efficacy of the decision options that you're discussing, you should also think about (and maybe talk about) who is helped and how by each of the options.

- **Longing to belong.** People driven by a need for affiliation and belonging, at work and in life in general, want to be a part of groups that share their interests—groups that accept them and want them to participate. This acceptance gives them a feeling of being a part of something worthwhile, a feeling of not being alone, and a feeling of validation. For any given interaction, look for affiliation implications that might be worth pointing out.

Don't pigeonhole these types of internal motivation as good or bad, per se. They can all be healthy, within limits.

We all have multiple motivations, and you can't be expected to constantly think about them all. Your boss's motivations will wax and wane depending on the their situation, but through observation you can see the one or two motivators that dominate their behavior. That's valuable information when you want to connect or persuade. Any issues that you might want to discuss with your boss can be analyzed and shaped through the lens of their primary motivations. If your boss is, say, considering vendors with whom to partner, who to hire, or options for an internal policy or process, then ask yourself which decision they'll be most comfortable with given their dominant motivation. In time, you'll be able to know which decision will likely be most valuable to you in terms of your relationship with your boss. Note that this isn't manipulation, which implies negative intent. Here, you're framing your interactions in a manner that respects your boss's major drives, building rapport and a stronger relationship.

Understanding Your Boss's Expectations

The biggest way to ensure that your boss looks favorably upon your work is to understand what is expected of you. The first thing to do is to stop assuming that you know what your boss is thinking. Your boss's expectations from your previous performance evaluation discussion might not be as clear as you think, depending on:

- Your communication skills

- How well your boss prepared for your evaluation

- How much things have changed since then

To clarify what's expected of you, be proactive. Be prepared for your evaluation. Assume that your boss will miss something and be ready to fill them in. After your evaluation, follow up once in person (not three or four times, just once). When you drop in to see your boss, reiterate your priorities as you understand them, and tell your boss not to hesitate to check in with you if priorities change.

Be respectful of your boss's time: after the informal check-in following an evaluation, wait for at least two months. Checking in more often than once every few months could make you seem like you're trying too hard to manage your boss (which isn't the goal here).

Getting answers to the following types of questions can clarify your boss's expectations:

- What are key ways used to judge the overall performance of your team?

- How will you be personally evaluated in your role as leader?

- What near-term milestones must be completed?

- What new or upcoming milestones must be completed or launched?

- What key metrics will be used to examine your team's outputs?

- Do you have training to complete the core required aspects of your job?

- Does a problem employee need to be addressed?

- Does someone need to be hired?

Also, address "good citizen" behaviors such as:

- Mentoring your team members
- Joining a professional association
- Serving on a planning committee for an upcoming event

What you're expected to do is largely dictated by your job description, employment contract, evaluation, and other documents, but remember that interpreting the different facets of performance can be subjective, and that sometimes priorities change. Never let your boss be surprised by what you're working on or how you're progressing. Every week or two, send your boss a simple, short email that gives a quick update or FYI. This way, your boss will always know what you're up to and can push you in a new direction if necessary.

If you remember to stay in touch and think through the different aspects of performance, then staying on top of your boss's expectations will become an easy, normal part of your monthly routine. And your boss will be happy because it shows that you want to perform at the highest level.

Choosing Communication Channels

What good is a well-crafted message if it's delivered poorly? To connect effectively with someone requires not only a thoughtful message and communication skills, but the proper medium—usually called a communication channel—through which you send your message. If you choose the right channel, your boss will be attentive and more likely to listen. If you select a suboptimal channel, you risk having your message muddled.

Before you choose a channel, first decide whether your message should be delivered privately or in the presence of others. The short answer is to err on being private. Others may see you as manipulative if they witness you filtering information or asking certain questions, and that can harm you over time.

The major communication channels are:

- **Face-to-face.** Most of the time, opt to communicate face-to-face. The capacity for information exchange is huge and you can clear up any confusion or misunderstanding immediately.

- **Telephone.** This channel is convenient and permits certain nonverbal cues, such as tone of voice. Also, you can leave a voice mail.

- **Video conferencing.** This channel is somewhat more inconvenient than the telephone but in many ways it rivals face-to-face communication.

- **Email or text messages.** Email and texting are efficient and provide a record of the exchange. Unfortunately, they tend to be overused, adding to the pile in your boss's inbox.

- **Handwritten notes.** Actual physical notes written on paper or post-its are personal and unintrusive. When your boss finds them, they create a reassuring feeling that you're staying productive.

Don't overuse any particular channel. For urgent or sensitive messages, use the fastest available high-quality channel (face-to-face works best, then telephone). For confidential messages, the best channel is always face-to-face.

Being Helpful

Managing up is a positive activity, not a negative or manipulative one, and being helpful is one of the best ways to ensure that, in the long run, the people you're helping will be willing to help you. This applies to your boss more than anyone else.

Nothing is more helpful to your boss than having an employee who meets or exceeds expectations consistently. Being helpful can also mean providing physical assistance (making copies or putting up party decorations) or intellectual assistance (proofreading a report, auditing a spreadsheet, or providing a different perspective). If you see something or come across a bit of information that you know your boss will find useful, make a note and deliver it.

You can also advocate in your boss's absence. Suppose that you and the team have been tasked with hiring a new colleague. As the process unfolds, based on what you know about your boss and the direction the team is going with the decision, you might want to speak up and make sure your boss's view is heard and considered (without equating the boss's view with your own).

Helping your boss yields several benefits:

- Increased comfort and rapport in your interactions
- Higher levels of trust
- Greater likelihood that your boss will consider you for new opportunities

Amidst all this helping, be sure to share your future goals and aspirations with your boss, making it known that you don't plan to stay and be wingman forever. A short conversation every four or five months will suffice.

Helping Your Boss Make Decisions

Making decisions is fundamental to what happens at work and so must be part of managing upward. Sometimes that just means acting like a sounding board and giving your boss a fresh perspective when you're asked for it. Other times that means moving a step further to better highlight the path you feel is most advantageous.

The simplest way to help your boss make a decision is to offer fresh information or perspectives. Suppose that your boss is considering a policy change on how expense accounts are approved. You think that she's correct, but you wonder whether she's considered the effect on morale because she's been managing expense accounts with little oversight for years. So you mention to her that if she takes that route, she'll have to be sure she doesn't appear to be micromanaging or suggesting that people have been irresponsible or dishonest. Your boss may or may not change her view based on your input, but the way you framed it supports her position while also offering food for thought that questions the decision, or at least offers insight into framing and selling the decision.

In the preceding example, you were just trying to be helpful, with no desire to persuade your boss to follow through with the change or to reverse course. But in some decisions, you'll have an option that you like best among the choices that your boss is considering. If you believe that multiple good decisions exist but you like one in particular because of your interests, then you can act on that preference to a limited extent. Position your preferred option effectively, without advocating for or speaking negatively about the other options. Be careful not to withhold relevant information or fudge numbers in support of your preferred position. The effective tactics for advocating a favored option are:

- Make it feel like your boss's idea

- Appeal to higher-level goals

- Cite organizational values

- Use advantageous data or statistics

- Speculate about others' reactions to the decision

Making Promises

Making promises is a consummate example of an act where the desire to do right can create an unintended bad outcome when things go wrong. Your boss tells you that the client wants the report by Friday. Or that you can't work any overtime until the end of the month. You want to help your boss, so you make a promise because you think that you can deliver. You say, "Yes" or "No problem" or "I can do that." That's a promise. The only thing more explicit is actually using the phrase, "I promise." And making promises can lead to serious problems:

- Breaking a promise is breaking your word, and that can have a huge effect on how others view you. Making a promise is easy. Breaking a promise and making up for it is hard.

- People on average are bad at estimating their odds of success for a given task. We typically underestimate how much time it will take and how likely it is that other things will pop up and compete for our time.

- We typically make promises under a particular set of circumstances and then those circumstances change. You thought that you could do what the client wanted, for example, but then the client called you and asked for something more or something new.

Strenuously resist making overt promises while still striving to ensure your boss that you'll get the job done. When things change, even if it's not your fault, and you can't keep your promise, two bad things happen immediately:

- You create negative emotion. People don't like finding out that something they were counting on isn't going to happen. That negative emotion affects you, and others, in many ways.

- You lose some social standing with your boss. Your reputation takes a hit. Respect accorded you declines.

Breaking the rare promise causes minimal damage. But repeated offenses will quickly harm your relationship by changing how your boss thinks about your future. Your future assignments, evaluations, and promotability all can suffer as bits of unflattering data accumulate in your boss's mental file.

Promises don't pose much of a threat when you use them rarely and only under the right conditions. You can use them for tasks or projects of small or modest importance, for example. But never make promises for big, important issues. If you commit to some task and your boss says, "So I have your word that this will get done?", then do not say, "Yes." Instead, look him in the eye and say, "I'll do everything in my power to get this done. Don't worry." If he presses the issue, say, "If it can be done, I'll do it. OK?" Eventually, your boss will come to understand the dangerous nature of promises.

If you consistently deliver high-quality work on time, then you'll be meeting expectations and making your boss happy. He won't expect promises because he knows you'll do the work.

Promoting Yourself

The workplace systems designed to hold you accountable and to evaluate, reward, and promote you are imperfect. Your boss and the other leaders in the organizational hierarchy are very busy. Your boss, peers, and team all are continually bombarded with information from all directions. From these facts it's clear that you must actively manage the impression that others have of you and your work. You somehow must claim your mind share to ensure that people remain aware of what you're doing and, more important, what you're accomplishing.

We all know people who have caused themselves problems by taking things too far. They talk about themselves and self-aggrandize too often. They become known as brown-noses or kiss-ups who can't wait to tell the boss about their amazing work. No one likes such people. They're self-centered, insincere, and often lack integrity. Your goal is to promote yourself appropriately so that your efforts result in a boss and peers who value you.

The key to self-promotion is knowing what to promote, when to promote it, and how to promote it. Most people think that they're supposed to promote themselves to the boss and others only when they accomplish some big project successfully. That's untrue. You can self-promote only so many times before you're labeled a self-centered kiss-up, so don't waste those opportunities on accomplishments that your boss is already aware of.

Your big wins are seen by everyone, so you should focus on the smaller, unique wins that you create. Examples of small wins that you might want to share with your boss include:

- You make a great contact at a prestigious potential client.

- You complete a high-profile project several weeks ahead of schedule.

- You tweak a process that shaves a full day off one of your core tasks.

After you decide what to promote, you must choose when. Here's the rule: self-promote a win to your boss *when* it happens, but no more frequently than once per quarter, or you risk being viewed as too self-focused.

After the what and when comes the how. To promote yourself effectively:

- **Share credit.** Occasionally promoting group wins and the individual wins of others makes you appear to be interested in the team, not only in yourself.

- **Promote only evidence-based wins.** If there's no sale, email, report, or something that clearly shows that you created the win, then promoting that you did becomes dangerous. Be sure that your role is clearly evident.

- **Vary communication channels.** Sometimes talk face-to-face, sometimes send an email, and sometimes leave a handwritten sticky note (page 106). Don't overuse face-to-face meetings, which can be seen as too aggressive for this type of communication.

In the end, you are your biggest and most dependable supporter, so you must find ways to speak up and be sure that your accomplishments are known, without inadvertently creating problems for yourself.

Responding to Feedback

Every time that you interact with your boss, you're making an impression and promoting yourself, whether or not you're referring to your accomplishments overtly. You can think about self-promotion from a different perspective—not when you're telling your boss something, but when she is telling you something. Specifically, when she's giving you feedback on some aspect of your performance. The more difficult the feedback is, the more your reaction will speak volumes about yourself. How you deal with challenging feedback can make a huge impression.

If you don't like your boss's feedback or if you feel like you're being attacked unfairly, never attack back. Reacting to negative communication with your own negativity never helps you and often hurts you. Suppose that your boss unexpectedly tells you that she thought your presentation to a client was flat. Specifically, she says that you took too long, seemed unsure of several details, and lacked the energy to keep the client interested.

You're not used to this type of feedback, and you have three sensible ways to respond:

- **Keep quiet.** Say nothing, nod, listen, and take a few notes if it feels appropriate. This tactic is often a smart move—particularly if your boss is worked up and clearly has things that she wants to say, and nothing you have to say really matters in that moment. Remain attentive and respectful, but quiet. In terms of managing your boss, this reaction shows that you're able to listen and are emotionally intelligent enough to be quiet and take a few notes.

- **Say a little.** Interact just a little with the goal of honestly trying to understand your boss's feedback without challenging it. Safe things to say include brief replies like, "OK. I think I understand that," "I appreciate your feedback," and "When you said I was a little boring, was it my content or my delivery?" Don't overplay your hand—say just enough to get a few details. Show that you're listening, own up to your performance, and signal your intent to improve. In terms of managing your boss, this reaction shows that you're strong enough to take tough feedback and smart enough to want to improve.

- **Challenge politely.** Politely challenge your boss if and only if you're confident that you're correct. This tactic is risky. To pull it off, you must be unemotional, completely noncombative, and willing to let it go if your boss disagrees. A polite disagreement might go like this: "The sale might not be lost. I know that we wanted to close the deal today, but they did say that they wanted to deliberate, so it might happen." Or this: "I admit that it wasn't my greatest performance, but it was because I was trying to show humility rather than overconfidence." No matter what you say, always end with something like, "But maybe you're right. We'll see how it plays out, but I do appreciate your feedback." You can assert yourself by suggesting that interpreting the issue at hand is subjective or a difference of opinion. But be quick to admit that maybe your boss is right, and you did come up short. And always thank your boss sincerely for the feedback. In terms of managing your boss, this reaction shows that you can walk the line between accepting feedback and respectfully standing up for yourself.

Use one of these tactics when you receive tough feedback, and you'll survive unscathed. You may even be able to turn a tough moment into something that actually helps you.

Documenting Issues

Your boss is busy. Sometimes he thinks that he's being clear when he's not. Sometimes he's clear in the moment but later forgets what he said. These miscues are normal and happen frequently, but they won't necessarily cause you problems if you've learned when and how to document certain decisions and interactions. Documenting certain things is useful for three main reasons:

- When others who are involved in the task understand that a meeting or conversation has been documented, their commitment tends to increase because documentation often functions as an informal contract.

- When others see you documenting something (a meeting, for example), you're signaling to them what your next move will be. In some ways, you've written a script that everyone has agreed to follow. They may or may not follow through but at least you've signaled your intentions.

- Documentation serves as a method to cover yourself in the future. If you document a meeting, for example, should anyone down the line question why you did something, you'll have a credible document of how your boss or the team made certain decisions and you were simply following through as expected.

Documenting *everything* is a poor way to manage your boss, however. If you constantly document and reiterate everything that goes on around you, then you'll drive people crazy, especially your boss. Instead, document only the most important things—that's about 20% of the events, exchanges, or conversations where you and your boss are involved.

If appropriate, you can follow up by giving your boss a summary of your documentation. Vary your approach. Don't always show up at your boss's office the day after the big meeting to reiterate the four main takeaways. You can do this once in a while, but sometimes send an instant message, write a post-it note, or send an email. Just find some way to show your boss that you understand your marching orders and to signal your next move.

Another popular approach is to use regularly scheduled pushes (updates) that document what's been decided and what you're up to. A sensible practice is to send a status email every two or three weeks. This message should document what you're doing and why, reiterate the relevant directives given to you from your boss, and summarize your progress. These regular updates reduce the likelihood that you'll surprise your boss. Furthermore, when your boss gets a snapshot of your activity, he may realize that he's been unclear or wants you to change course.

Avoiding Tricky Issues

Managing upward is often straightforward, but there are a few situations to avoid:

- **Upstaging your boss.** Doing so is understandable in some ways, but almost always a bad idea. You recognize in the moment that you understand something or know something that your boss doesn't, but instead of biting your tongue or sharing privately, you blurt it out like a classroom know-it-all. As a result, you make your boss (and possibly others around you) look unprepared or dumb.

- **Overagreeing with your boss.** "That's a great idea, boss. I couldn't agree more. My thoughts exactly." Such people are called yes men (or women). Some yes men are trying to win approval and influence the boss. Others are simply being too nice in deference to the boss's higher status. In either case, they're shooting themselves in the foot. Nine out of ten bosses don't like this behavior. They'd rather have employees who respectfully share their real opinions.

- **Throwing your boss under a bus.** You blame your boss for something when speaking to someone else. It doesn't matter whether you're talking to someone else on your team or someone outside of the team. Never badmouth your boss. It rarely stays private and it's always viewed as disloyalty.

- **Interrupting.** Nothing shows a lack of respect more than cutting off people when they have yet to finish their point. When you do this to someone above you, you lose their respect.

- **Do what you said you'd do.** You'll fall out of favor with your boss if you repeatedly say that you'll do A and then you do B. Even if the path you chose was productive, you're behaving inconsistently with what you said.

- **Being supercritical.** You don't want to be a yes man, but you don't want to be the opposite either: someone who's overly argumentative and critical of the boss's ideas. Every boss is different. Your goal is to find the balance between these two extremes that feels appropriate for your boss.

- **Leaving your boss out of the loop.** Help your boss *not* to be surprised or unprepared. If you have info that you know your boss will value, and you're not sure whether she knows about it, then find a fast and simple way to clue her in.

Working With a New Boss

Sometimes, even though you're not the boss, you might have to do some boss-like work. That's particularly true when you have a new boss, who might be a first-time manager or simply new to your department. In either case, your new boss will need some help learning the ropes, giving you a special opportunity to manage the boss.

Never let your new boss wonder exactly what you're up to. Take extra care to share the scope of your work and where you are in terms of major milestones. Also, if he requests it, sketch out the rest of the team as well so that he can get to know the players and how they work together. As the first few days pass, don't assume that your new boss knows exactly what he's doing with regard to all the key processes and tools that define your group. No matter what his level of expertise, he won't know the exact way that your team processes its work, deals with clients and internal customers, or uses certain tools.

Check in with your new boss every few days to ask him how he's settling in and to remind him that it's OK to ask you questions. After you establish some rapport, you might share additional work-related information, such as a short history of the group or the group's relationship with other departments. Be positive. Don't point fingers. Be honest when describing the environment, but don't delve into messy politics. Don't describe who likes/hates who, where the camps and coalitions are, who helped who, and who caused trouble for who. Your new boss can feel that out for himself. If you start telling stories, true or not, you'll mark yourself as a person with loose lips, a person who may lack integrity, or even someone not to be trusted.

If your new boss asks you about politics, tell him that you weren't really involved in that issue and maybe he'd get better information from the people who were involved. Your hands stay clean and he's likely to respect how you handled the question. On the other hand, feel free to tell him about the problems that pop up repeatedly so he'll be prepared instead of surprised. For example:

- An annoying customer who always calls on a particular day of the month

- A department with whom you often argue about resources

- A report that goes to the CEO that always causes debate

Within the first few months of your new boss's tenure, make sure that he knows your long-term aspirations. After about four or five months, he'll have learned about the responsibilities and performance of the team and its members, including you. Initiate a conversation about your goals and aspirations. Keep it short, informal, and lighthearted. Save the formality for your annual evaluation discussion.

Working With an Unavailable Boss

An unavailable boss is closed instead of open and interactive. She doesn't check on you, send regular emails to keep the team in the loop, keep her door open, and so on. Think back over the previous year. If you've been seeing a lot of unanswered emails, unanswered phone messages, missed meetings, and unexplained office absences, then you have an unavailable boss.

The risks of having an unavailable boss are:

- You risk not being recognized when deserved

- You risk not knowing about certain things coming down the road that will affect the team

- The team risks not receiving the proper support that they need to get the job done

A boss will adopt this management style for three main reasons (from most to least likely):

- **Personality.** Your boss is wired to be quiet, restrained, and cut off. When personality is the biggest driver of behavior, taking the actions listed below often helps significantly.

- **Your boss doesn't like you.** You two don't have good chemistry or mesh well. In this case, assuming that your boss is important to your professional future, you can craft a conversation that will let you two talk about it. Only then can you start to work on whatever the core issues are.

- **Crisis.** Your boss is dealing with a personal or professional crisis. In this case, you're likely to know that a crisis exists because being closed off isn't your boss's typical style. The only thing you can do is check in. Tell your boss that you haven't heard much from her lately, and ask whether there's anything that you can do to help.

Here are three actions that are likely to help:

- **Talk.** Talk to your boss, not about the work tasks, but the actual communication issue. Be kind, positive, and respectful. In all but the rarest cases, your boss will respect your move and will be likely to try a little harder.

- **Be proactive on your own.** Don't pester your boss or go see her to talk about every little thing. Focus on the minority of things that you're working on that are most important to your boss. And for those, send a short weekly email or just stop in to chat.

- **Set a schedule.** Ask your boss whether she'll chat with you or, if appropriate, with the team every day for five minutes or every week for a half hour. Discuss it and find your own solution. If you put a conversation on the calendar, it's much more likely to happen.

Working With a Boss You'll Never Like

The difficulty of working for a boss that you don't like depends on how bad the relationship is. It could be as simple as feeling uncomfortable or as bad as feeling panicked, worried, or constantly angry. You can:

- Cope with the situation, or

- Manage it actively

Coping encompasses the rituals and habits that you form to live with the relationship as-is. If you're sure that you lack the power or skill to engage your boss and change the relationship, then focus on coping for as long as needed. If the relationship is defined by ugly behavior directed at you, and you're having trouble sleeping or concentrating, or you're feeling depressed, then you're smart to start a job search and find a way out.

A toxic relationship will affect you physically if you stay in it too long, but coping may work well if the relationship is only mildly dysfunctional. Here are some coping tips:

- **Never fan the flames.** Don't speak negatively to or about your boss, lest it come back to you and make an ugly situation worse.

- **Stay away.** Keep your interactions to an absolute minimum. Don't socialize. Have no unnecessarily long professional conversations.

- **Engage in positive rituals.** Create at least one or two positive response behaviors to use every time that you're about to melt down after an interaction with your boss. Eat a small piece of chocolate. Call your best friend for five minutes of venting and laughing. Develop small rituals to remind you that your life is bigger than your relationship with your boss.

If you want to manage the issue actively by talking to your boss and facing the issue head on, then first consider the risks. Before you act, think carefully about your odds of getting your boss to open up and have a positive conversation about your relationship. If you proceed, remember to own the problem, frame it as an opportunity, avoid negativity, and suggest a path forward. A proper opening statement might be:

> *"Lately I've noticed that things have been tense between us. We have friction sometimes, and I think that perhaps I create a lot of that. I know there's been a few times where I've been harsh. And I wanted to say rather than not say it. You're my boss and I respect you. But I think that if we can talk about this now or clear the air every once in a while, then maybe we can enjoy working together a little bit more. I hope I'm not off base here. Does this make sense?"*

State the issue without going into specific details. Be positive and respectful from the start. With the right attitude and carefully chosen words, you can take an important but damaged relationship and make it better.

Working With a Remote Boss

In today's workplace, your peers and boss may be located in a different building or country. Advances in communication technology have given rise to virtual teams, where you might work in an office or at home. Either way, most of your colleagues work elsewhere and you're connected only electronically. Sometimes, the team all works in the same place and it's only the boss who's virtual.

You can manage an absent boss by using these tactics:

- Be explicit about your expectations and your boss's expectations. In a positive manner, tell your boss the two or three things that you need from him in terms of communication and support that will help you thrive without having him in the office. Maybe that's being copied whenever a particular topic is being discussed, or maybe it's permission to act on a particular issue without having to check with him. Also, ask your boss what he needs from you so that he won't get nervous and start wondering what's going on in the office. It might be a certain report by a certain time, or some other form of communication that keeps him in the loop.

- Regardless of your boss's stated expectations, schedule regular pushes. Pushes are updates that you send to your boss to keep him in the loop. You probably need to do this only once each week. Schedule it just like a meeting. Your boss will come to count on your consistent updates.

- Communicate regularly via real-time video. You have only so many times to connect with your virtual boss, so get the most out of each encounter. A high-quality video connection is as close to face-to-face communication as you can get, and much superior to audio-only channels.

- Meet in person one, two, or three times each year, where one person travels to see the other. Face-to-face meetings reveal facial expressions and body language. In-person communication has maximum impact.

- Use team huddles. When the boss is virtual, it's easy for him to hear (rightly or wrongly) different or conflicting messages from various team members. Meet with the team regularly to discuss how to communicate with the boss. Agree collectively on the topics and positions that the boss needs to hear, and by who and when. Individuals can still contact the boss at will, but the team needs to be sure that no one is stepping on someone else's toes unknowingly.

Working With a Self-Important Boss

A self-important boss has an inflated and unjustified positive self-image. Often, a disposition toward arrogance and self-importance limits such a person's growth in an organization. The tell-tale signs of a self-important boss include:

- She thinks that she's ultimately responsible for every good idea and win that happens in the office. When someone else says something interesting or does something impressive, she instantly tells you why something that she did actually led to the other person's success.

- She's sensitive to status and often reminds you that her status exceeds yours. She drops the names of executives with whom you don't interact. She speaks of her personal parking space. She mentions her bonus when she knows that you don't get one. She's happy to do these things in front of other people to reinforce your lower position in the hierarchy.

- She enforces double standards. She admonishes people who show up late though she often is late. She enforces a dress code that she violates herself. She asks people to work weekends but never works weekends herself.

Unfortunately, this behavior is driven by personality, and you can't change someone's personality. If your boss's behavior is embarrassing or in breach of company policy, then you can speak to Human Resources. Otherwise, your goal is not to manage your boss but rather to plan your escape.

While you're still trapped with your boss, be careful not to inflame the situation:

- Never encourage your boss to pontificate more

- Never over-toot your own horn

- Never directly or negatively respond to self-important behaviors

Let it all roll off you and move on. But pay attention—you can learn more from bad bosses than good ones.

Your escape plan can be a multimonth or multiyear search for a new home elsewhere in the same company, in a different company, or in your own business. Grow your personal and business networks to ensure that your opportunities increase.

Working With an Incompetent Boss

The more competent you are, the more likely you'll encounter a boss at some point that you feel lacks competence. Inexperienced or unskilled bosses can spring from various sources:

- They rise to their level of incompetence. The Peter Principle states that organizations promote people into management positions based on their skills in their current role rather than on the skills needed at the next level.

- The person is a political appointee or is a friend or relative of someone in power, and thus has benefitted from favoritism, nepotism, or something other than merit.

- You're working in a low-performance workplace that's dominated by low accountability and mediocrity.

No matter how your boss arrived, he's your problem now. Compounding the stress of working for an incompetent is the fact that his performance and reputation can rub off on you. Fortunately, you have ways to manage the situation:

- Don't talk bad about your boss. If he discovers that you're questioning his ability, then he'll distance himself from you. And, counterintuitively, you must stay close to him to minimize the damage that he causes.

- Avoid going over your boss's head. Doing so will anger your boss and could be seen as disrespectful by your boss's boss for not using the chain of command. If possible, work with your boss to ensure that his weaknesses don't cause problems.

- An incompetent boss will tend to delegate to you tasks that he doesn't understand. A sensible strategy is take this tendency a step further. After a few months of covering for your boss, you might be in a position to ask for a promotion or a raise. Document your work well to use as leverage. (Don't let yourself become a habitual target for delegation without receiving any credit.) Find time prior to your next evaluation to discuss with your boss your aspirations for the next few quarters. Your boss needs to know what you expect.

- Once in a while, mention your contributions to your boss's boss. Be casual and matter of fact. Don't report your boss's shortcomings. Mention only a milestone achieved or a project that you wrapped up, thus subtly indicating the level of work that you're completing. If your boss discovers that you've done this and has a problem with it, then you can stand your ground to prevent him from stealing the credit. Or you can cave and say nothing. The best choice is usually to find the comfortable spot between these two reactions, depending on your relationship with your boss.

Working With a Mean Boss

Mean bosses are nasty or inappropriate. They don't usually last long because even weak companies often self-correct to get rid of such people. Even so, there's no shortage of them, and they come in two flavors:

- Bosses who break policies, laws, or otherwise make you miserable
- Bosses who are merely annoying and awkward

If your boss uses profanity, makes inappropriate comments, demeans you in private or in public, or acts violently, then you may be in what labor lawyers call a hostile work environment (a form of harassment). It doesn't have to be violent or sexual. It could be as simple as repeatedly asking you to do inappropriate personal favors (get my lunch, run an errand, babysit my kid). If you think that your boss might be reasonable about it, you can just take the risk and speak up. Just say, "Can we talk about something else?" or "I'm sorry, I'm busy that evening." If your boss takes the hint, maybe the behavior will end there. Otherwise, document the issue and then go to a labor lawyer or to the Human Resources department. Remember that if HR pursues the issue, then your boss will find out it was you, so be prepared.

The more common type of mean boss is annoying and awkward. You're not losing sleep, you're not getting an ulcer, and no laws are being broken, but it's still no fun. These types of bosses tend to:

- Share nonwork, off-color, or personal opinions that they should keep to themselves.

- Adopt a critical attitude. Every time that you see your boss, you know that a little negativity is coming your way.

- Not like you for reasons that you may not understand, manifested through critical comments or exclusionary moves (such as not inviting you to certain meetings or events).

The first step in dealing with an annoying and awkward boss is to distance yourself appropriately. Choose not to interact any more than is absolutely required.

If the problem involves a specific type of personal interaction, try to redirect your boss any time that it occurs. For example, say, "I'd rather we just talk about how to wrap up this project, OK?" Don't name the inappropriate thing that your boss was doing—just ask to move on. If the issue is exclusion and the meeting or event that you're missing is important, you must speak up quickly to correct the behavior. If you need to go further, your only options are to address the actual issue or seek help from Human Resources.

When in doubt about whether your boss will honestly listen to you and care about your feedback, try to speak to him. If you're dealing with this more common type of annoying and awkward behavior, then you don't want him to later accuse you of failing to do the obvious. Talk to him. Choose a safe time, in private. Be positive and concise. Give one or two real examples without being accusatory or judgmental. If this doesn't work, your last resort is Human Resources.

To increase your odds, consider taking more members of the group with you to speak to your boss or even Human Resources. Generally speaking, the more people you have, the stronger the message.

Repairing a Damaged Relationship

Even strong relationships can sour in many ways (upsetting comments or decisions, disagreements, general dislike). Many times you won't feel compelled to address a damaged relationship, but if it's important to your professional future, then try to repair it.

If you have any doubts about the status of a relationship, ask yourself these questions:

- Has the frequency of interaction with the other person clearly decreased?

- Has the other person stopped using you as a resource?

- Has the other person stopped including you on various types of reports, emails, or other forms of communication?

You may also have direct evidence of damage based what the other person has said to you. If you're convinced that an important relationship is damaged, swallow a little pride and choose to deal with it. Take the high road and apologize, show an act of good faith, and agree to communicate more in the future. An appropriate opening line might begin with:

> *"I feel like you and I have started going down the wrong path, even if neither of us meant to, and we've started getting on each other's nerves. I've noticed that I get too critical, too quick with you. And you've started to tune me out..."*

Meet in the other person's office to set a friendly tone. Jump right in and name the issue. Own up to the fact that you helped create it. Put forth a show of good faith (a favor) that entails some small risk to yourself. Wrap up by suggesting that you meet like this again.

Next Steps

The better your boss is at being a leader, the less you'll need to think about managing up. Good leaders are naturally inclined to keep you and your needs clearly on their radar. You'll still find times when you want to be proactive, but the burden is small when you're working for a competent boss.

You can start managing up right now by planning your first unscheduled check-in that you're going to initiate with your boss.

Choose:

- One update to give your boss

- One longer-term issue to discuss

- One question to ask about a third topic

Do it today, if feasible. Knock on your boss's door, pop in your head, and ask, "You got three minutes?" Sit down, be concise, take a few notes, and thank your boss for the time when you're done.

As you move up the hierarchy, you can develop more-advanced upward management skills, such as:

- Coaching others in your professional network to manage up.

- Indirectly managing up. That is, managing your boss through your relationships with people who you're both connected to. People such as your boss's boss, your boss's peers, other key personnel in the company, key clients, and so on. The more your boss hears about you from these important people, the greater your mindshare.

- Encourage your direct reports to manage *you*. What can you say, to whom and when, that will signal to your team that you're open to a productive, two-way dialogue? The more you engage in open, pro-employee behaviors, the more they'll feel comfortable talking about their thoughts and aspirations.

In the end, managing up is about trying to help your boss while also actively trying to create the future that you want. It might feel odd at first, but take it slow. In time, you'll build a better relationship with your boss—one that's mutually beneficial and instrumental in moving you to the next level.

CHAPTER 10

Managing Conflict and Repairing Relationships

Despite our best efforts, we find ourselves in difficult situations almost every day. Our happiness and success in life and the workplace depend on the quality of our relationships and our ability to cooperate. With the right set of skills, you can repair or preserve your relationships with your coworkers, clients, family, and friends.

This chapter shows you how to resolve conflicts by using simple, repeatable techniques and best practices that apply to most business and personal situations. Along the way, you'll learn how to navigate from conflict to cooperation by identifying divisive issues, separating the people from the problem, and overcoming barriers to resolution.

The Conditions for Conflict

Conflicts occur continually in our lives but we don't consider them to be troublesome until they escalate into disputes. In our relationships with others, we often have conflicting goals, values, needs, and wants, in tandem with unequal access to resources and differing moral stances. A dispute arises from conflict when three beliefs collide:

- You're being deprived of something that you need or want

- Someone else is depriving you (blame)

- That deprivation violates a social norm

For example, Bob forgets to include his boss Alice in an email loop regarding a new project that he's pursuing. Alice becomes upset about being omitted. She accuses Bob of violating the workplace rule of manager approval. Her accusation starts a cycle that escalates into a dispute. Deconstructing this dispute in terms of the three conditions listed above, we have:

- Alice feels she's been deprived of something she wants

- Alice blames Bob for the wrongdoing

- Alice claims that Bob has violated a social norm

Recall your most recent argument with a friend or coworker, and try to deconstruct the conversation. (Even if the argument occurred in only your head, it's still a conflict—an internal conflict.) If you haven't had a full-blown argument recently, consider something that you're upset about now but have yet to air. Now, answer the following questions:

- What was the issue?

- Who did you blame?

- What solution (expressed or left unsaid) would resolve the issue in your favor?

- If instead you were on the receiving end of the argument, how did you react?

Completing this inquiry creates a framework for seeing the conflict clearly, one that you can use as a personal working example throughout this chapter.

Responding to Conflict

We all have ingrained, culture-driven ways of responding to conflict, regardless of the scenario. Understanding these responses builds awareness and enhances our capacity to make better choices under fire. The most common ways to deal with the discomfort of conflict are:

- **Suppression.** Forbidding or restraining the discussion of an idea, activity, or issue. We refuse to talk about certain things, and we tell others that they shouldn't talk about them either. We shut down any possible resolution because the whole process makes us uncomfortable.

- **Avoidance.** Refusing to talk to someone with whom you've had a dispute. We don't give voice to our true thoughts or feelings. Instead, we stew, we harbor bad thoughts, we have imaginary conversations in our heads, or we talk to someone else, trying to gain alliances and prove we are right and the other person is wrong.

- **Resolution.** Finding an agreement that both parties can live with. We're engaged, making an effort to understand why the conflict occurred, and brainstorming ways to solve the problem cooperatively.

- **Transformation.** Using the conflict to explore your relationship with the person with whom you're having the dispute in a way that resolves the conflict and transforms your relationship. We work to understand that the other person is actually a partner in the conflict. We summon the courage to own our part in the conflict with the intention of changing our behavior in a lasting way.

- **Transcendence.** Consciously moving through and past a conflict, free of bitterness and resentment. We're no longer dominated by the need to repeat the conflict. We've given up the hold that our triggers have on us.

How you choose to respond to a conflict generally follows a progression. Without conflict-resolution skills, we tend to alternate between suppression and avoidance. The more effort you expend in resolving conflicts over time, the more confident you become in your ability, and the more likely you'll devote your time to resolution, transformation, and transcendence.

If you already operate somewhere between resolution, transformation, and transcendence, then you're ahead of the game. On the other hand, if you opt for suppression and avoidance, then start paying attention to your triggers (the things that typically upset you). Your default response to conflicts will change the quality of your relationships—you can't resolve a conflict unless you're willing to take your part in it.

Contentious Tactics

If we're not skilled in problem solving, we often resort to contentious tactics during a dispute. That is, we try to resolve the conflict on our own terms without regard for the other side's interests—we hold steady to prove we are right and they are wrong.

Contentious tactics are all attempts to manipulate the other person. In the absence of conflict-resolution skills, it's doing whatever you need to do to win. Learning to recognize these tactics increases your self-awareness and ability to notice when others are using them against you. This awareness will give you the opportunity to pause, slow things down, and choose a more cooperative approach. The most common contentious tactics are:

- **Ingratiation.** Getting what one wants through charm or flattery or being likeable. This tactic is useful and most appreciated when it's authentic. "Hey, you're really a better editor than I am. Would you take a look at this document?"

- **Promises.** Getting what one wants now by agreeing to do something later. This tactic is most useful when used for mutual gain, rather than as a power play. "I promise to take you to lunch in return for covering for my shift."

- **Shaming.** Expressions of dismay, shock, or disapproval of another's behavior, usually on moral grounds. This tactic is much more common than is usually admitted, and it can destroy relationships. "Your work is embarrassing and you're not living up to your potential."

- **Persuasive argumentation.** The use of logic and reason to change somebody's behavior or position. This tactic is often used to prove that the other person is wrong or to lower the other person's expectations. This tactic rarely succeeds because convincing someone to do something they don't want to do often backfires, despite your impeccable logic.

- **Gamesmanship.** Getting what one wants by pushing the rules or ratcheting up the stakes, like forcing a foul in basketball. The sole purpose of this tactic is to come out ahead. "If I have to give you ten days notice, I'll give it to you at 5 P.M. on Christmas Eve."

- **Threats.** Getting what one wants by threatening to cause the other person harm if they don't comply. Threats can vary from subtle to frightening and be delivered via any communications channel (email, face-to-face, the rumor mill, and so on). Remember that threats and accusations are pleas for help. "If you don't submit your report, you're going to have to work over the weekend."

- **Physical force (violence).** Hitting, pushing, shoving, taking, throwing, war, terrorism. Norms, rules, and laws that govern our behavior are broken.

Recognizing these tactics is of critical importance if you're to teach people how you want to be treated. Calling attention to the tactic as it happens puts the other person on notice that you won't play the victim. Most often, they will acknowledge their misstep and return to cooperation.

Recall your most recent disagreement through the lens of contentious tactics. Recognizing your own preferred tactics is a step forward in choosing a constructive alternative.

Cognitive Biases

Cognitive biases are illogical thoughts and inferences that operate below the surface of our awareness to cloud our judgment during disagreements. These buried thought patterns often cause us to cling like barnacles to our positions in the heat of a dispute. Scores of cognitive biases are studied (see Wikipedia's list at *en.wikipedia.org/wiki/List_of_cognitive_biases*). Here are some common ones you'll encounter in conflict resolution:

- **Hindsight bias.** The tendency to view past events as being predictable. "I knew it all along." When Alice accuses Bob of intentionally excluding her from an email thread, Bob might respond, "I knew you'd have that reaction and wouldn't support me."

- **Fundamental attribution error.** The tendency for people to explain the behavior of others as personality defects, while minimizing the role of situational influences. Alice views Bob's failure to keep her in the loop as underhanded or political—a personality defect—rather than as forgetfulness or busyness (or an unconscious reason).

- **Confirmation bias.** The tendency to look for or interpret information in a way that confirms our preconceptions. Alice's view that Bob is out for himself is confirmed yet again by his failure to include her.

- **Self-serving bias.** The tendency to take more credit for successes than failures, and to interpret events in a way that benefits our interests. Bob explains how his individual accomplishments make him a great fit for the new project, while minimizing the effect that the extra work would have on his current responsibilities.

- **Belief bias.** We form an opinion about the logic of an idea or proposal not on its merits, but on our belief in the truth or falsity of the conclusion. Believing that more is better, management pushes to produce more product, rejecting any proposals favoring quality over quantity.

In reality, we have endless implicit and explicit biases and beliefs about ancestry, ethnicity, gender, nationality, economic status, interests, weight, appearance—you name it. Even though we lack sufficient information to know with certainty why people act or think in the way they do, our brains are wired to judge and find meaning. In the absence of facts, our brains work fast to pigeonhole things in ways that fit our perceptions of reality. Cognitive biases developed in response to human evolution in a dangerous and confusing world, so it's unlikely or impossible to eliminate them in ourselves or others.

To discover your own biases, visit Harvard University's Project Implicit (*implicit.harvard.edu/implicit/takeatest.html*) and take one or more of the Implicit Association Tests. If you recognize your own biases, then you can step back from them and better perceive the other person's perspective. This self-awareness can help you defuse—or altogether avoid—a conflict.

The Principles of Influence

In our everyday conversations and disputes, we use what social scientists call Principles of Influence. Understanding these principles and consciously choosing them helps us regain our balance during a dispute and claw our way back to cooperation. The principles of influence are:

- **Reciprocity.** People are highly motivated to return a favor or good deed, or respond to a positive action with another positive action. As a social norm, if you're treated kindly, you're much more likely to respond with kindness, rather than self-interest. If you're treated with hostility, you're likely to match that hostility or worse. As Alice and Bob try to resolve their misunderstanding, Alice might agree to make herself available for career development advice, while Bob might respond by running new opportunities by Alice first. Using reciprocity requires knowing what you want and what you're willing to give in return.

- **Commitment and consistency.** If people commit, orally or in writing, to an idea or goal, then they're more likely to honor that commitment because establishing it is congruent with their self-image. Consistency is really about integrity. After we commit to something, we have a strong drive to do what we say we're going to do. That's why we're motivated to make good on financial agreements or to meet deadlines.

- **Social proof.** People will do things that they see other people are doing. Social proof is conforming to custom or group behavior. You're more likely to put a tip in the jar if there's already money in it, or work overtime on a project if the whole team is doing the same. In the workplace, you can jumpstart social proof by getting an influential person to support your promotion or idea.

- **Authority.** People will tend to obey an authority figure (like a boss or professor), even if they're asked to perform objectionable acts. Power isn't solely vested in someone's title or position, however. We also align with authority by the brands we buy, the cars we drive, the clothes we wear, and the people we associate with. We also use authority when we cite statistics or use testimonials or customer feedback to give our product or service credibility. In the workplace, you can claim more authority by networking with influential people in the organization.

- **Liking.** People who are similar to us are more likely to be influenced by us. In the workplace, if you're a mother, then you're more likely to connect with and trust other mothers.

- **Scarcity.** Perceived scarcity will generate demand. In advertising, for example, saying that offers are available for a "limited time only" encourages sales. In the workplace, scarcity can take the form of urgency. If you're trying to get a project approved, you might stress the impact that acting immediately will have on the competition or the bottom line.

All these principles can be used to deceive or manipulate, or they can be used to help guide people to take positive action. Become a student of human nature. Seek to understand what motivates people to act and use the principles of influence to collaborate.

The Path to Resolution

The social psychology of conflict explained in the preceding sections is useful for expanding your self-awareness and bettering your understanding of others, but now it's time for actual strategies and solutions. The rest of this chapter develops a set of practices (a series of steps) that you can use to resolve conflicts. The steps are:

- Identify the issues

- Build trust

- Ask diagnostic questions

- Reframe the problem

- Brainstorm

- Come to an agreement

Before you proceed, prepare and practice by writing down five of your own behaviors that you'd like to change, especially when you see those same behaviors in others. These are your triggers.

Next, recall a recent argument you had with a boss, coworker, or family member. Somebody did something, and you got upset, perhaps very upset. On a scale of 1–10, 1 being only mildly irritated, and 10 being the highest level of intensity, how irritated (triggered) were you?

Now, rate on a scale of 1–10 your capacity to deal with your emotions for this issue. A 1 means that you're so triggered by this problem you can hardly speak about it. A 9 or 10 means you have a lot of room for the feelings that come up around this issue.

If you're a 9 on the irritation scale and a 3 on the capacity scale, for example, then the distance between these two numbers suggests that you have to build your capacity to deal with this conflict (or, more generally, this type of trigger).

Suppose that Alice repeatedly takes credit for Bob's work. For this issue, Bob's a 9 on the irritation scale and a 3 on the capacity scale, meaning he's extremely frustrated and doesn't understand how to deal with his frustration. The wide gap between how intensely he's triggered and his low capacity for dealing with those feelings suggests that Bob isn't likely to try to resolve this conflict. But, short of quitting, Bob's only way to reduce his stress and improve his workplace relationships is to face this conflict.

You can use the practices detailed in the following sections to build your capacity to transform your relationships. *You* are the agent that affects change by controlling your own responses—you can't change other people and it's pointless to try. As the gurus say, it's never about the other person, even when it is.

Identify the Issues

When we're in the midst of an argument, we often don't know why or how we got there because so many arguments begin over trivialities. The real issue is buried out of sight.

Suppose that Bob is under pressure at work. He's been doing subpar work and missing deadlines. He's afraid that Alice will fire him if he doesn't improve. And he sees Alice as a hypercritical micromanager. How did Bob and Alice move from avoidance and blame to such a dire state? When we're in a blaming state of mind, acknowledging the conflict and being willing to talk about it is by far the hardest step in resolving it. Finger-pointing keeps you in an endless cycle of blame with little hope of uncovering the real issue.

To help pass this roadblock, do these three tasks before you even sit down to resolve the issue:

- **Identify the nature of the disagreement.** Is it relational, having to do with your relationship? Or is it substantive, a disagreement about content or process? Or is it perceptual, a disagreement about how you are viewing a situation?

- **Investigate your own interests.** If you identify that your disagreement is over process (how something gets done), then also identify what values, preferences, or needs you perceive are being thwarted.

- **Schedule a meeting.** After you've completed the preceding two tasks, ask for a conversation with the other person. Schedule it so you have plenty of time and privacy, do it face-to-face or at least voice-to-voice, and stay wary of cognitive biases (page 131) clouding the issue.

Alice doesn't know whether Bob's collar is too tight and making him irritable, or whether he's buried in administrative work and needs an assistant. If Alice assumes anything, it should be that Bob's actions aren't directed at her personally. Her assumption is key.

Once you are both at the table, your first task is to identify the other person's interests. To do so:

- Listen to the other person even if you think that you already understand their perspective. If you listen without interjection and counterpoint, very often you'll discover information that helps solve the entire issue.

- Confirm your understanding by paraphrasing or restating what the other person says. If you're unclear, say so, and keep at it until you are clear.

Beginning is for many people the most difficult part of the process. Gather your courage and be the one who takes the first step towards resolution.

Build Trust

After initiating a conversation with the other person, commit to collaborative problem solving. That is, make every effort to move through the discovery phase of the conversation without assigning blame. To do this, you must build trust and create an atmosphere of possibility. Here are some guidelines for building trust:

- **Manage yourself.** If things get heated, pause and slow things down. When you resume, speak in a measured tone, even if the other person can't. They will likely match your conversation style unconsciously.

- **Don't blame.** The language of blame begins with "you," "he," "she," or "they." The language of responsibility begins with "I." Take personal responsibility. Say, "I am angry," instead of, "You make me angry." Say, "I am afraid I won't be heard," instead of, "You never listen to me."

- **Active listening.** Active listening is paramount in conflict resolution, especially when tensions run high. Let the other person vent and give them time, ask them to let you rephrase uninterrupted what you're hearing. Practice active listening in your everyday conversations. Listen without interruption and repeat what you hear. You may find that it transforms your relationships.

- **Focus on the present.** If the other person dredges up incidents from the past, redirect the conversation back to the present. You might say, "It seems like we're drifting off-topic, we were talking about missing deadlines, let's go back to that."

Even when you're certain that the other person is the wrongdoer, take responsibility for your part in the conflict; otherwise, you run the risk of staying trapped in the conflict cycle. Regardless of the issue, focus on your commitment to a mutually beneficial outcome. Repeat a stock phrase like, "I'm sure we can solve this," to demonstrate your commitment and keep trust high.

These are guidelines, not inviolable rules. Bounce between them as needed throughout your conversation. At this point, you have a sturdy but hopeful beginning to the conflict-resolution process, one that's hard on the issue but soft on the people.

Ask Diagnostic Questions

At the heart of conflict resolution is a technique called diagnostic questioning. Diagnostic questions are open-ended, usually starting with words like who, what, when, where, why, and how, or phrases like, "Tell me more about…". If you ever get stuck, ask diagnostic questions to help you understand the issues from the other person's perspective and discover what their needs, preferences, and goals are.

Open-ended questions are most effective when you run into objections or flat-out refusal. They let you dig a little deeper and create an atmosphere of mutual problem solving. In the absence of facts and information, we tend to mind read and make assumptions, or worse, we try to convince people to do something they don't want to do. Asking diagnostic questions helps you gain clarity and guide the conversation toward a mutually satisfying resolution.

Statements and assumptions can be turned into questions. For example, "Tom put you up to this." becomes the open-ended question, "Who else has an interest in this issue?" And "Your idea will have a terrible effect on customer service." becomes "Who might be harmed as a result of this idea?"

Be careful of using "why" questions like, "Why did this happen?" or, "Why do you need that?" Even though such questions often get to the heart of the matter, they rely heavily on your tone of voice and nonverbal cues that can be easily misinterpreted as judgment or accusation, particularly if you're on delicate ground. Instead, see if you can substitute "why" with "what" or "how" questions. For example, rephrase, "Why do you need that?" as, "How will this help you?"

Sample Diagnostic Questions

To help you master this technique, use the following list of sample diagnostic questions as a cheat sheet. If you get stuck, remember: who, what, when, where, why, and how.

How would you characterize the issue/problem?

Who do we need to include in the conversation?

Who might be harmed as a result of this issue?

How can I help you avoid that harm?

Where do you think we might get more information that would help us resolve this problem?

Would you like me to search for that information?

What's most important to you?

What's least important to you?

What would be the best outcome for you?

What's difficult about X?

How can I help you?

How do you see our relationship evolving if we resolve this issue?

What do you fear might happen if we don't resolve it?

What's holding you back?

Where do you wish you could go?

What would you do if your hands weren't tied?

If we were partners in this, how could we use our strengths to support each other?

What role would you like me to play in resolving some of the problems you're having with X now?

What's upsetting you?

What do you think is fair?

Why do you think that's fair?

What about that resolution seems fair?

What else?

What might be left unsaid or undone?

Tell me more about....

Reframe the Problem

Framing creates perspective. If you recall your most recent disagreement, you may have framed it as a contest between right and wrong, setting the stage for a downward spiral into name calling. Instead, reframe the problem in a more optimistic light, being soft on the people but hard on the problem. Skilled framing encourages you and the other person to search for fresh solutions to old problems, move from anger to understanding, and shift from victimization to empowerment. Here are some framing strategies:

- **Move from fighting to problem solving.** If you're in a heated argument, then pause, slow things down, and lower your voice. And then ask the other person to step back from the fight and see the task at hand as a problem-solving session.

- **Move from being right to being happy.** If the other person is stuck on being right, shift the focus to the interest that you're both trying to serve. You might make lists of what you're each trying to accomplish and then see whether any of those goals overlap. Follow that with ideas or actions that can help you reach those goals.

- **Move from uncooperative to cooperative.** You're the only person whose behavior you can control, so pull back and focus on the bigger picture. If the other person digs in, ask diagnostic questions (page 137) to bring them back into cooperation. Say something like, "It looks like we've hit a wall, help me understand what happened." If the other person is willing to re-engage, then you'll discover something that will help you reframe the issue and give you an opportunity to brainstorm (page 141) solutions that benefit you both.

- **Move from potential gain to potential loss.** Counterintuitive as it may be, framing the dispute as a lose–lose proposition resolves more fights than framing a proposed solution as win–win. The potential of losing $10000, for example, is a bigger motivator than the potential of making $10000. We don't want to lose what we already have.

- **Move from past to future.** Don't get hung up on the past—getting agreement on past events is almost always impossible. If you did or said something that was offensive, apologize and make amends by agreeing to be a better communicator in the future, starting right now.

Framing Examples and Exercises

To defuse an active dispute that has come to focus more on the people than on the problem, try reframing the problem by using the following examples as a guide.

Example 1:

Frame: "Your subpar work shows that you don't take your job seriously."

Reframe: "I'm doing the work of three people and it would be helpful if you'd prioritize so I know where to focus."

Example #2:

Frame: "Dave has bad time-management skills and is constantly interrupting me."

Reframe: "Dave may need some direction and clarity to help him be more productive."

Now, reframe the following statements to turn the conversation around.

"If I say no to my boss, I'll get fired."

"The marketing people don't understand how the product works."

"The only reason Sally gets to work at home is because her kids are always sick."

"Your resume indicates you don't remain long in any given position."

"Why should I hire you when I can get everything you offer for free on the internet?"

Brainstorm

Brainstorming is an inquiry with the purpose of investigating ideas and making proposals that lead to solutions. Brainstorming relies heavily on diagnostic questions (page 137), so it's also a powerful tool for discovering mutual interest as well as common values and experiences. Brainstorming can help you in the early stages of conflict resolution to flesh out issues and needs. To structure your brainstorming process, do the following:

- **Before you tackle solutions, explore your mutual needs.** If you focus on the solution too early, you won't get to the core need or problem. A problem defined in terms of needs opens up the possibility of a win–win solution. "What do you need to be happy?" is a good place to start, or, "What roadblocks are you running into on this project?"

- **Rule nothing out.** Throughout your brainstorming session, focus on quantity, not quality. Don't stifle creativity by evaluating any idea or debating its practicality or probability of success. You'll have time later to cherry-pick the winners.

- **Expand on each other's ideas.** Your best resolutions often arise from tacking a new idea to an existing one. Resist competing. Let yourself be inspired.

- **Let your ideas go.** We tend to angle for our own ideas, even if they're half-baked. Let them go. Don't be derailed by being stubborn about a particular idea or solution. Often that's what got you into the conflict in the first place.

- **Start with easy stuff.** When you're identifying the issues, you may end up with a long list of things to resolve. Start with the easy issues first, and you'll be rewarded more quickly. You'll build on the trust that you established early on and give one another good reason to hope that the more-difficult issues can also be resolved.

- **Improvise.** Go with—not against—what the other person presents. Say yes, and then follow that yes with more ideas, something that moves the story forward. If you reach an impasse or you feel at a loss for the next step, take a break. And when you come back, pull out your diagnostic questions and improvise from the question: Where might we go from here?

Come to an Agreement

By this point in the conflict-resolution process, you've accomplished a great deal. You have:

- Identified the issues

- Created an atmosphere of trust and possibility

- Asked diagnostic questions to discover your own and the other person's interests

- Brainstormed potential solutions

The final step is coming to an agreement (resolution). If you've brainstormed well, you have several ideas or proposals to consider. The best outcome from your mutual effort is for you and the other person to walk away feeling heard, accommodated, clear about next steps, and possibly happy.

To get that kind of result, focus on consensus, not compromise. These two words are not synonyms. Consensus is considering proposals and choosing solutions that satisfy the highest number of mutual needs and interests. Compromise is usually associated with giving up something, often grudgingly, leading to a semiwin–semiwin rather than a win–win.

Reaching consensus still requires give-and-take. As you consider different proposals, you'll be making concessions and asking for reciprocity. But your guiding intention must be consensus, or you run the risk of returning to the same argument because your true needs weren't met. To test for consensus, throughout the agreement process, ask a few stock questions: Does this proposal meet our mutual interests? Are we both happy with this idea?

Conflict resolution is stressful, so it's easy to walk out of the room and forget important details. But the durability of your agreement depends on its specificity, so write down the details for finalizing every point of agreement, including:

- What processes, actions, or deliverables are you committing to?

- What's the timeline for completing those actions or deliverables?

- If it's an ongoing process like a periodic meeting, when will it happen?

- How you will communicate your progress?

Finally, confirm your understanding by reading back your agreement to the other person, and later follow up with an email that reiterates the same information.

Before you walk away from the table, thank the other person and acknowledge their persistence, cooperation, and commitment. Whether you've just solved a family squabble or a disagreement with your business partner, you've both done something uncommon that made your world a little better. It's not often that people set aside their egos and fears to work out a problem.

Barriers to Resolution

Ultimately, other people are opaque to us. We have no idea why they act or think as they do until we ask. But what if, despite all your efforts, you keep meeting resistance? What if all the evidence shows that it really is the other person? When you're not successful in solving a problem with a difficult person, you could be dealing with incomplete information. Unspoken interests may lie beneath the surface.

Suppose that Bob thinks Alice is a difficult person. He believes she doesn't support his goals and aspirations, never acts on his salary requests, and micromanages his every move. What Bob doesn't know is that Alice may have hidden constraints, stakeholders, decision-makers, interests, or values. Maybe Alice is hindered by the constraints of Human Resources policies. Or she lacks the authority to meet Bob's requests. Or upper management has put a ceiling on spending.

To dig deeper into the other person's interests:

- **Clarify confusion.** As soon as you notice that you're losing track of the conversation, acknowledge that you may be missing something or that you're confused about the reasoning behind something. You could be talking past one another, and you need to pause and ask for clarity. When you understand why someone is resistant or irritable, it will usually point you in the direction of a solution. If the other person is angry because they're misinformed, inform them. If they're angry because they feel disrespected, respect them. If they're frustrated because they misunderstood something you said, clarify and correct the misunderstanding.

- **Summarize your conflicting stories and harmonize your differences.** When we get locked in conflict, we're usually bound tightly to our story. We provide circumstances, conversations, past events, and other evidence that supports it, and the other person does the same. If you both can see clearly, then you can summarize your conflicting stories and adopt a new story. Discern where you're in agreement and where you have shared values and goals, and then use those shared values as your guiding principles in your resolution process.

In the end, don't let your assumptions and interpretations of people and events overwhelm you. Go to the source and seek clarity. Dealing with difficult people is about understanding what else might be operating underneath. Uncovering hidden motives, summarizing conflicting stories, and harmonizing your differences has a potential silver lining: your perception of the other person as a difficult person may change completely.

Next Steps

It's easy to tell yourself that the other person is difficult, rude, abusive, or manipulative. And that may be true. But conflict resolution requires you to adopt the view that it's never about the other person, even when it is. That's easier said than done, but you now have a set of practices to help you move from assumption to clarity to resolution.

Conflict Resolution Cheat Sheet

Identify the issues

- Identify the nature of disagreement: Is it relational, substantive, or perceptual?

- Investigate your interests: What are your values, priorities, preferences, goals, etc.?

- Listen.

- Paraphrase what you think the other person is saying.

Build trust

- Manage yourself.

- Take personal responsibility (use "I" language).

- Listen actively.

- Focus on the present.

- Take your part.

- Express your commitment to resolution.

Ask diagnostic questions

- Turn statements (accusations) into open-ended questions: who, what, when, where, why, and how.

Reframe the problem

- Move from fighting to problem solving.

- Move from being right to being happy

- Move from uncooperative to cooperative.

- Move from potential gain to potential loss.

- Move from past to future.

Brainstorm

- Explore needs before solutions.

- Focus on quantity, not quality, of ideas at first.

- Rule nothing out.

- Expand on each other's ideas.

- Let your ideas go.

- Start with the easy stuff.

Come to an agreement

- Examine proposals for satisfaction: do they meet your mutual interests?

- Write down specifics.

- Capture the processes, actions, or deliverables you are committing to.

- Specify the timeline for completing those actions or deliverables.

- Determine how you'll communicate your progress and close the communication loops.

- Read the agreement to the other person.

- Follow up by email.

- Appreciate and acknowledge the other person.

CHAPTER 11

Working for a Toxic Boss

Few people outside your family affect your life more than your bosses do. Over the course of a varied career, you might have 15 or more bosses, and even more if you include all your bosses' bosses, who can act like you report to them directly. Most of these bosses will be decent managers (and decent people), but some of them are going to be toxic, which can harm you and your team.

The Effects of a Toxic Boss

Toxic bosses may or may not have great work skills, but their values, personality, or interpersonal skills drive you to tears. A toxic boss is someone who:

- You don't respect or enjoy

- Threatens your mental well-being and professional progress

- Consistently acts inappropriately toward you or others

- Is overwhelmingly critical of your work and the team's work

- Shows clear ethical lapses repeatedly

Unfortunately, when you come face-to-face with a toxic boss, it's easy to choose the path of least resistance by doing and saying nothing in response to your boss's behaviors. This type of conflict avoidance is understandable—who wouldn't want to get away from a difficult person

147

immediately? Folding may seem like a sensible tactic in the moment, but ultimately it's not a smart choice because it can cause persistent problems. The longer that you're associated with a toxic boss:

- The more your accomplishments fade in the minds of others

- The more likely you'll become trapped in your current position for a long time

- The more your reputation will become tainted as the two of you come to be regarded as a pair (guilt by association)

- The more likely you'll have mental and physical problems such as cognitive fatigue, difficulty focusing, difficulty thinking deeply, persistent negative thoughts, and even induced physical fatigue in your boss's presence

- The more your burdens and fatigue cause your performance to suffer

- The more your reputation and the quality of your other relationships suffer, hurting your long-term professional potential

A toxic boss is just one of the many things in life that you have to deal with that aren't your fault. Fortunately, you can be proactive, mitigate the damage, and create a plan to move on. These are skills that anyone can learn, and this chapter shows you how.

The Source of the Problem

Only when you become clear about the root cause of a problem can you react properly. Here, you want to clarify your thoughts to the point where you can articulate why your boss irritates you.

Above all, beware of your volatile emotions. Don't assume that you know what's causing the problem. When you make simple assumptions in difficult situations, you're sacrificing effectiveness for efficiency and likely making things worse. Instead, slow down and contemplate the four likely causes of your situation:

- **You.** You may be saying, "I'm not the problem." Maybe you're not, but I guarantee that you don't see yourself and your behaviors as clearly as you think you do. That's a fact of life confirmed by years and volumes of research. You may be contributing a little or a lot to the situation. Swallow your pride and turn your analysis inward. Honestly consider whether you've exacerbated or helped create the problem yourself.

- **Your boss.** Consider each of the following:
  - ▸ What your boss says to you and others around you
  - ▸ Specific boss behaviors that cause friction
  - ▸ Instances of poor work performance by your boss
  - ▸ Ethically questionable or illegal behaviors that your boss engages in

  Now ask yourself whether many things or only one thing typically bothers you. Be as clear as possible before moving forward.

- **The interaction between you and your boss.** Sometimes you have real issues. Sometimes your boss has real issues. But other times neither of you is the problem individually—it's when the two of you interact that sparks fly or things get tense. It's common for two normal personalities to not mesh well, and recognizing this makes it both easier to cope and easier to be proactive in addressing the issue.

- **External factors.** Various outside factors might be huge stressors in your life or your boss's life. Perhaps there are tensions in your group caused by performance or budget problems. Or maybe bigger issues within the company are straining everyone's relationships. Be careful not to allow external stressors to negatively influence how you view your boss—it's unfair and it won't improve the situation.

The more clear you are about what's causing the strain between you and your boss, the more likely you'll be able to figure out how to deal with it effectively. You must be able to articulate the root cause before you can create an action plan.

Types of Toxic Bosses

Many types of difficult bosses exist. The absent boss, for example, is always unavailable and hard to find. The workaholic boss never thinks that you're working enough hours despite your accomplishments. These people are certainly a pain, but the three most common toxic bosses are:

- **The Micromanager.** This boss hovers, checks in continually, and just can't let you go back to your work. The cause often isn't a lack of trust in you but the need to be in control. To give yourself room to breath, when you're given a task, calmly and concisely repeat the instructions back to your boss, instilling confidence that you understand your marching orders. Another simple tactic that often works, especially for larger tasks, is to proactively send electronic updates that keep your boss in the loop. Regularly scheduled updates can keep your boss from feeling the need to interrupt you at your desk constantly.

- **The Overly Critical Boss.** This boss provides consistent negative feedback, regardless of whether your performance is bad, good, or amazing. Maybe it's just a personality flaw, but you don't really care about your boss's motivation. If the critiques are personal, not just professional, and are delivered in front of others, then just discuss it with your boss privately if you don't fear repercussions for just speaking up. In other circumstances, the best solution usually is to avoid the risks and bite your tongue. Your boss—not you—has the problem. Keep your head down and spend your time working on a future that doesn't include your current boss.

- **The Incompetent Boss.** This boss was promoted to a leadership role for some reason other than leadership ability and work-related skills (nepotism, politics, the Peter Principle, or whatever). Your boss causes you ongoing problems by making mistakes and not understanding fundamental concepts. To come out of this relationship unscathed, be positive, help your boss, and never speak condescendingly. Soften your speech by using phrases or questions like, "Hmm, did we consider...?" instead of, "I think you forgot to...". You're trying to build knowledge and awareness, so never badmouth or blame, which only hurts and never helps in the long run. Be as helpful as possible while continuing to work on your long-term plan to move on.

You can't control your boss, but you can control how you react. Check your emotions, think about your options, and accept that sometimes you have to bite your tongue and let it roll off you. In the end, you can learn as much about leadership from toxic bosses as you can from exceptional ones.

Emotional Triggers

Dealing with a toxic boss sometimes bothers people so much that they stop thinking clearly. Logic and reflection go out the window as strong emotions take over. Don't let this happen to you. Controlling your reactions is a choice that starts with understanding and managing your triggers. A trigger is a specific type of recurring interaction you have with your boss that jerks you out of a positive productive mood and into a negative unproductive mood.

Think about the strongest specific triggers that happen during your typical work week. For example:

- An uncomfortable comment made during a meeting

- An inappropriate use of email

- A customer that your boss makes you deal with even though it's not your job

No matter whether your boss is a micromanager, overly critical, incompetent, or problematic in some other way, your goal is the same: reflect until you can articulate what the dominant triggers are, when they're happening, and why. Then (and only then) can you devise workarounds that help you avoid trigger situations while still getting work done. Some common workarounds are:

- **Use others as a buffer.** Have others with you during the interaction. If the trigger behavior is always in the boss's office, for example, have someone else present.

- **Let others handle the interaction.** Send a peer, a direct report, or even an intern. Don't send someone into an ugly situation, but if you believe that someone else could attend the meeting, hand off the report, or whatever, then try it (assuming you have the power to do so). Another person might simply have good chemistry with your boss.

- **Communicate electronically.** When possible, reduce face-to-face interactions by communicating electronically. This workaround works especially well when the trigger behavior happens only when you're both together physically. Provided you can exchange the right information and complete the task, opt for lower-quality communication channels such as email or text messages rather than telephone or video calls.

Evaluating Your Situation

How bad is your situation? Should you try to avoid your boss and do nothing, or should you try to speak up and manage the situation proactively?

To evaluate your situation, first consider its severity by putting it in perspective. Are you feeling mildly irritated two or three times a week because of your boss's behavior? Well, that's normal and not cause for alarm or action on your part. On the other hand, if it's happening nearly every day and you're bothered to the point of being unproductive, then you have a relationship issue that you can't ignore. When you leave work each day, are you:

- Unable to leave work-related thoughts behind?

- Having serious trouble getting your boss out of your head?

- Constantly talking to your friends or your spouse about it?

- Losing sleep?

- Dreading the thought of returning to work?

If so, you're in a highly severe situation. However, high severity doesn't automatically mean that you should engage your boss in a face-to-face discussion. Before doing so, ask yourself:

- How long will you be working for your boss? If you might be stuck there for years, then you have a large incentive to seek a solution.

- What is your relative power? Power and influence doesn't come solely from one's position in the organizational hierarchy. Based on work performance and personality, your boss may be less powerful or much more powerful than you at work. The closer or higher you are in status, the lower the risk of speaking up.

- Is the behavior in question directed at you or at nearly everyone? There is strength in numbers. Being part of a group that politely and positively has a conversation with the boss is generally safer than going it alone.

- What's the cost of doing nothing? If you avoid any action at all, what is likely to happen? Are you going to develop ulcers, feel depressed, and deliver low-quality work? Do you have any reason to believe that the behaviors might escalate? Will your inaction slow your professional progress?

In summary, the cost of doing nothing is high if:

- The behavior is severe

- The relationship with your boss could last for years

- You have a strong standing at work relative to your boss

- The bad behavior is affecting many people

Speaking up entails considerable risks, so think through each of these issues before you decide whether to do so. *How* to speak up is covered in "Speaking Up Effectively" on page 154.

Protecting Yourself With Documentation

Whether or not you eventually decide to speak up to your boss, you still need to protect yourself, meaning:

- Don't enable bad behavior

- Don't inflame bad behavior by your reactions

- Don't speak poorly of your boss to others

- Document your behaviors and interactions with your boss

You may never need documentation, but in rare cases you might be put in a position to verify what you did or did not say or do. The most important form of documentation concerns performance expectations and formal performance evaluations. Try to have all goals, tasks, and project expectations documented in forms or emails that your boss signs or responds to affirmatively. Regarding your evaluations, it's *your* responsibility to make sure that these documents adequately address all major aspects of your work.

Documenting questionable or negative behavior is more difficult. For extreme instances, you can see someone in Legal or Human Resources immediately. But for the vast majority of questionable behaviors, you're wise to not be rash. Assuming that no laws or important policies were broken, you simply want to document what took place for you own files. The main ways to do so are:

- **Get it in writing.** Have your boss acknowledge significant directives in writing. If you're told, for example, to quote a certain price, to use a certain vendor, or to not share information with someone who's normally in the loop, then get confirmation on paper or via email before you proceed.

- **Speak publicly about it.** Document via the use of public comments. The most common example is speaking up in a meeting to ask for someone's opinion about what you've been asked to do. Don't do it in a manner that suggests you have a problem with the task. Appear to be matter-of-factly looking for perspective or making conversation while you're actually broadcasting your secret (so to speak) to others. Your boss, if present, can clarify or change things if needed.

- **Keep a diary.** If your boss's behavior is outright hostile, such as being profanely or excessively insulting, then keep a simple diary. Record what was said or done, when, where, and who else was present. You may never need it, but not having it may someday put you in a tough spot unnecessarily. Document only events that you witness firsthand. Secondhand testimony can be used to make you look like an unreliable gossip.

If you start documenting your interactions, be sure not to jump the gun or be too judgmental—you're looking for genuinely unacceptable behavior that is beginning to appear in a pattern.

Speaking Up Effectively

Suppose that you've followed the advice in this chapter so far, and you've decided to speak up and address your boss. Two types of risk are involved. One type of risk is that you've failed to adequately understand behavioral triggers (page 151) or keep proper documentation (page 153). The other type of risk is associated with how you craft and deliver the actual conversation. You can't know exactly how your boss will react, but you can improve the odds of receiving a productive response by knowing how to structure the interaction.

Focus on three issues:

- **When to have the conversation.** The best time is when you know that your boss's calendar contains no regularly occurring meetings, visiting clients, or other predictable distractions. Also avoid meeting when any projects that your boss is overseeing are in crisis mode. Wait until your boss's workday appears to be relatively uneventful, then schedule the meeting in person, not through an administrative assistant or email. Show respect by dealing with your boss directly. If you're uncomfortable doing this, you likely shouldn't have the meeting. If you're asked to sit down and talk then and there, be ready to have the conversation.

- **How to frame your message.** Be observational, not accusatory, and specific, not general. For example, don't say:

  "You're always hovering over my desk and it's bugging me."

  Instead, say:

  "I've noticed that you've been checking in with me frequently. Is there a problem I should be aware of? You checked in with me nine times last week on the Microsoft account, so I was just wondering if there was anything that you wanted to discuss."

  The first statement is too short, lacked specificity, and is too negative. The second statement is specific, respectful, and asks for performance feedback.

- **Use a light and positive tone of voice.** For example, don't say:

  "You're really bothering me."

  Instead, say:

  "I've noticed that you're checking in a lot lately."

  Tone, like framing, matters because how you say things is as important as what you say.

If you follow these three rules, then you probably won't feel compelled to actually ask your boss to stop the behavior, because the point will have been made without the actual asking. In fact, if you feel the need to ask explicitly because your boss isn't getting the message, then you probably shouldn't ask. To go any further is quite risky, and your best bet is to bite your tongue and end the discussion gracefully. Continue documenting, and if the behavior persists and is severe enough, consult Human Resources.

When to Seek Help

It's sometimes necessary to speak to someone other than your boss about your boss's behavior. Violating the chain of command can be quite risky, so consider these factors before you decide:

- **Duration.** How long has the difficult behavior been taking place? In general, if the answer is a few weeks, then do nothing. If the answer is many months, then consider taking action. If the answer is multiple years, then you're actually at fault for doing nothing for so long, and making a change can be quite difficult. Many months is the best answer for several reasons:

  - ▶ It's long enough for you to have confidence that the behavior is a pattern, not just a blip.

  - ▶ It's long enough for your boss to become self-aware about the behavior.

  - ▶ It's long enough to show that your boss is unaware, or aware but uncaring.

- **Severity.** Is the behavior public or private? If it's public (insulting you in front of others, for example), then the severity is high. Your boss is not only causing you mental anguish, but also potentially hurting how you're viewed in the eyes of others.

In terms of how you're feeling, how is the behavior affecting you mentally and physically, in both your professional and personal life? If the situation bothers you modestly, but only while at work, then it's not severe. If it bothers you a lot at work and at home, to the point of harming your personal relationships or causing physical problems (ulcers or loss of sleep, for example), then the severity is high.

- **Outlook.** In the next year, is there reason to believe that you'll continue to have to deal with this situation? Might you be promoted or transferred to a different position away from your boss? Is there any reason to believe that your boss might be leaving? The more likely it is that you're going to have to stay with your current boss, the greater your need to seek help.

- **Scope.** Does your boss's behavior mainly affect only you, several people, or everyone? If the scope is wide, then the need to act is greater because so many additional people are involved. In this case, consider banding together to deliver a group message, because sometimes there is strength in numbers.

- **Who.** Who should you contact? One logical choice is your boss's boss. This is risky, but it's less risky than going straight to Human Resources, so be ready with a concise documented case. If you go to HR, know that your boss will find out, and you don't know how your boss or others will react when they find out. That shouldn't necessarily stop you, just be aware of the complications. The safest first step is to speak to your mentor for informal advice. A more experienced and connected person can help you put your options in perspective, and possibly save you from unnecessary headaches.

Next Steps

You've thought through the issues, the players, and the risks. Now, it's up to you. In a nutshell, here's how to proceed:

1. Think through the duration, severity, and scope of the problem. Be thoughtful and honest. Estimate duration to the month. Be conservative when estimating severity and scope. Don't assume that your boss is treating others poorly. Only rely on firsthand observation. If the situation has been causing you to lose sleep for 12 to 18 months and is also affecting some of your peers, then it's time to act.

2. Write down the names of your peers who might form the group willing to talk to the boss. Ask yourself whether you and your peers are experiencing your boss's difficult behavior at similar levels of severity. Some people have thicker skin than others. Also, consider whether they have the character to take this risk. We all vary in terms of how much risk we can tolerate.

3. Think critically about the team, department, and organizational culture. Do you work in a place that would actively listen to you and the case you wish to make? For some organizations, the answer is a clear yes. For others, it's questionable. Look for evidence of established grievance policies or cases similar to yours that have received proper attention. Lacking that, it's less likely your work culture will be receptive to the conversation you wish to have.